A Son is Revealed

Discovering Christ in Mark

Harry Uprichard

D1464620

 EVANGELICAL PRESS

EVANGELICAL PRESS
Grange Close, Faverdale North Industrial Estate, Darlington, DL3
0PH, England

First published 1999

British Library Cataloguing in Publication Data available

ISBN 0 85234 418 X

Printed and bound in Great Britain by Creative Print and Design
Wales, Ebbw Vale

Contents

Acknowledgements

Sincere thanks are expressed to all who have helped with this book: to Mrs Daniel McKee for her time, patience and care in typing the manuscript; to my friend and colleague Rev. R. N. McAuley for suggestions and proof-reading; to the staff of Evangelical Press for undertaking the venture; and to my wife Maisie, for all her love and encouragement in writing.

Harry Uprichard
Trinity Manse,
Ahoghill
January 1999

A Son is Revealed

Introduction

'Read Mark's Gospel', we often say, either to those who have just come to faith in Christ or to those who are interested in the gospel. I remember giving that advice to a young man who had just become a Christian. The result was remarkable. When I called to see him again, he mentioned how helpful Mark's Gospel had been. There he had found real people living out their lives, their joys and difficulties in real situations — people and situations that he could relate to. Mark's Gospel presents a story that races from one account to the next with hardly enough time to catch your breath in between. I was glad that I had given him that advice.

Mark's Gospel is short, clear and vivid. It is an action-packed eyewitness account where Christ is sharply and uniquely portrayed. The contents of the story are similar to those of Matthew and Luke, but the presentation is very different. There is a directness, an immediacy, a visual quality which grips the reader. It is as though the life of Jesus is flashed before us through the zoom lens of a TV camera, capturing instance after instance of Jesus' daily routine. The overall effect is one of growing wonder and astonishment. In his unique style, Mark addresses the burning question: 'Who is this Jesus of Nazareth at the heart of the Christian message?' This is a question as important today as it was in Mark's day, and as it will be on that great day when all of us will have to give an account to God himself of how we answered that question.

Mark, probably the John Mark of Acts, appears to have been particularly close to the apostle Peter. Peter describes him as 'my son' at the end of his first letter (1 Peter 5:13). Papias, the early Church Father, quoting an older contemporary, 'the Elder', comments: 'And the Elder said this also: Mark, having become the interpreter of Peter, wrote down accurately whatever he remembered of the things done by the Lord, but not, however, in order.' This suggests that behind Mark's account is the eyewitness testimony of Peter. Put at its simplest, it conjures up the view that as Peter spoke Mark wrote. There are also intriguing links between Mark's presentation of Christ and Peter's perception of Christ, as recorded in Acts and in 1 and 2 Peter.

As we look through the book of Mark, it is my heartfelt desire that all may be gripped afresh, as Peter obviously was, by the Lord Jesus Christ presented in the Gospel. In Peter and the other disciples we see men who were eyewitnesses of the Christ whom Mark presented. We see Christ himself tearing history in two, bursting into their lives, becoming the very reason why these men lived, served and died. This is the Christ that Mark would have us meet in this Gospel.

1.
Revealed Messiah

Mark tells his story directly. There is an immediacy about his approach. It is like a TV documentary, selecting the vital shots, getting to the heart of the issue. From the very outset of the gospel story, Mark is concerned to give a clear and crisp picture of Jesus of Nazareth — both who he is and what he did. There are no angels, no shepherds, no Joseph and Mary, no cattle-shed. Mark goes straight to the start of the good news. His opening words can not only be seen as a title of his Gospel but also introduce his entire theme: 'The beginning of the gospel about Jesus Christ, the Son of God' (Mark 1:1). That is what his story is about: the good news about Jesus Christ, the Son of God.

Where does the gospel begin? It begins with Jesus, the Son of God, who is 'Christ', the 'Anointed One'. 'Christ' in Greek means the same as 'Messiah' in Hebrew. The promised deliverer of the Old Testament is incarnate in the person of Jesus in the New Testament. Jesus of Nazareth is anointed by God for his life's work as Messiah. Mark then gives Jesus' title, 'the Son of God'. This means Jesus has deity; he is one with Jehovah. Jesus was not only the *promised* Messiah but the *divine* Messiah.

It is remarkable how much Mark says in this brief introduction. It brings us to both the source and the essence of the good news, for 'gospel' here means the 'good news'. Mark's summary approach anticipates all he is going to tell in his account. The fundamentals of the good news are all there at the very outset. Some claim that Mark wrote his Gospel for Christians at Rome. If this is so, then the growing clouds of persecution, which burst in the days of Nero and Diocletian, give added urgency to Mark's message. It is a story that he must tell as quickly and as clearly as possible. He begins with the revealed Messiah, promised by God and fully divine in his being.

Seeking

Mark's Messiah is a seeking Messiah. He is predicted in the prophets:

> It is written in Isaiah the prophet:
> 'I will send my messenger ahead of you,
>   who will prepare your way' —
> 'a voice of one calling in the desert,
> "Prepare the way for the Lord,
>   make straight paths for him" '
>
>   (Mark 1:2-3).

Actually there are two quotations here. The first is from Malachi 3:1. Malachi, the last of the Old Testament prophets, forecasts the return of Elijah before the Lord comes. Afterwards, the messenger of the Lord will suddenly come to his temple and cleanse it from all impurity. The second quotation is from Isaiah 40:3. A voice cries in the desert, preparing the way of the Lord, like a herald proclaiming the coming of a king.

The divine initiative

The remarkable thing about the predictions of these prophets is that they speak not only of a human preparation for the coming of God, but of a divine preparation for that coming as well. God sends Elijah to present the message. God himself cleanses the temple through the Messenger of the Covenant, his Messiah. God not only demands the levelling of the rough places, the raising of the valleys and the lowering of the mountains; he actually brings it about himself. God through the Messiah provides what he requires, gives what he demands, and initiates the preparation he seeks.

Calvin writes, 'When the spiritual truth is about to appear, John is sent to remove obstacles. And even now the same voice sounds in our ears, that we may prepare the way of the Lord: that is, that we might take out of the way those sins which obstruct the kingdom of Christ, and thus may give access to his grace. To the same purpose are the following words of the prophet: "The crooked shall be made straight" (Isa. 40:4). All that they mean is: there are intricate and crooked windings in the world, but through such appalling difficulties the Lord makes a way for himself, and breaks through, by incredible means, to accomplish our salvation.'

Salvation is not simply a matter of our coming to God; God actually comes to us. The Son of Man comes not only to save, but first seeks. Jesus takes steps to reveal himself to the hearts of those he chose out of sinful, wayward mankind, even before the world was created.

Mark makes that clear. He alone of the evangelists quotes from Malachi at this point in his story: 'I will send my messenger ahead of you, who will prepare your way' (Mark 1:2; cf. Mal. 3:1).

Messiah promised in the Old Testament

Why does Mark quote from Malachi as early as he does? It is not that Mark is mistaken and attributes to Isaiah an oracle really spoken by Malachi. These predictions were frequently grouped together in teaching about the coming Messiah and, of course, here the leading prophecy was that from Isaiah. It is rather that Mark wants to stress, in summary form, the breadth in prophecy of the divine preparation made for the Messiah's coming.

The Messiah's forerunner is not only Isaiah's 'wilderness voice' and Malachi's 'Elijah-type messenger' but even, to push the matter back further in Scripture, Moses' 'preparing angel': 'See, I am sending an angel ahead of you to guard you along the way and to bring you to the place I have prepared' (Exod. 23:20; cf. Isa. 40:3; Mal. 3:1; 4:5).

Mark shows how the whole of Old Testament prophecy, from start to finish, from Moses to Malachi, promises a Messianic forerunner. Mark shows that this forerunner is 'Elijah returned', just as Malachi foretold. Mark does this at the very outset, because the beginning of the gospel about Jesus Christ, the Son of God, originates in a Messiah who comes to seek the lost and to save. The initiative in salvation comes from a loving God who sends a seeking Messiah. That is why Mark gives John the Baptist so full an introduction.

Saving

Mark's Messiah is a saving Messiah. Introducing John the Baptist, Mark makes that clear. Mark first stresses the *similarity* between John's message and that of Jesus. In that sense, it is the beginning of the gospel. Mark gives the minimum of biographical details about John the Baptist. There is no birth story, no genealogy and no substance of John's preaching, as in Matthew and Luke. What Mark gives is a summary of John's message: 'And so John came, baptizing in the desert region and preaching a baptism of repentance for the forgiveness of sins' (Mark 1:4).

In his account, Matthew gives John's words directly: 'Repent, for the kingdom of heaven is near' (Matt. 3:1). That Mark should select this summary statement from among all the information he has about John is significant. It is not that Mark is ignorant of data about John. Indeed, later, he gives a full account of John's dealings with Herod and Herodias (Mark 6:17-29; cf. Matt. 14:3-12; Luke 3:18-20). Rather, Mark here chooses from his available information what suits his purpose — that is, to describe John's ministry as 'the beginning of the gospel about Jesus Christ, the Son of God'. That is Mark's point of emphasis.

What a remarkable summary that is! 'And so John came, baptizing in the desert region and preaching a baptism of repentance for the forgiveness of sins' (Mark 1:4). It focuses on the preaching as a priority, rather than on the baptism. The baptism is simply a visual aid, a sign and seal, a pointer towards, and guarantee of, the good news. It is an outward sign of an inner grace. Church ordinances must always take second place to the word of the gospel. They are subservient to it, explain its meaning and conserve its truth. Man is not saved through the sacraments, but through the message of the gospel.

Repentance

The summary stresses the negative thrust of repentance in connection with the gospel message. The 'about-turn' of the Hebrew word and the 'change of heart' of the Greek word for

repentance are both here. Old and New Testament are com-
bined. John's message is not simply about feeling sorry for sin,
but about *turning* from sin to God. Getting ready for the Messiah's coming involves that — a complete about-turn from
sin. Salvation begins as God acts upon the human heart, bringing about true and active repentance. 'Repentance unto life is
a saving grace, whereby a sinner, out of a true sense of his sin,
and apprehension of the mercy of God in Christ doth, with
grief and hatred of his sin, turn from it unto God, with full
purpose of, and endeavour after, new obedience' (*Shorter Catechism,* 87).

Sadly, much gospel preaching today lacks this note of true
repentance. People are urged to 'come to Christ', with little
explanation as to why they should come. The gospel is not
declared against the background of man's sin. So the real urgency of the call to repentance and faith is absent. An easy
'decisionism' replaces conviction of sin and produces superficial conversions. The beginning of the gospel about Jesus
Christ, the Son of God, according to Mark, requires repentance. The first words of both John and Jesus make that demand. We need to do the same today: 'In the past God over-
looked such ignorance, but now he commands all people
everywhere to repent' (Acts 17:30).

Forgiveness

Mark's summary also underlines the positive aspect of forgiveness of sins through the gospel: 'preaching a baptism of
repentance for the forgiveness of sins' (Mark 1:4). The prep-
osition 'for' makes this clear. John's preaching and baptism
were 'towards' that goal. Neither preaching nor baptism was
an end in itself. The end in view was the forgiveness of sins.

This fulfils all that the Old Testament has to say about forgiveness. The sprinkled blood on the door at the Passover, the

blood on the lid covering the ark of the covenant on the Day of Atonement, the elaborate ceremonial for cleansing the leper — all pointed to the expiation of guilt and the forgiveness of sins. Forgiveness is final and complete too: Isaiah spoke of God blotting out sins as with a thick cloud; Micah of God burying them in the depths of the sea; Jeremiah of God forgiving all sins and transgressions. The Day of Atonement depicted God covering over, indeed, obliterating Israel's offences. John the Baptist's preaching of the baptism of repentance pointed to the same — total cleansing from the consequences of sin and reconciliation with God. It anticipated the very heart of the gospel, which is that 'The blood of Jesus, his Son, purifies us from all sin' (1 John 1:7). Mark includes repentance, with a view to forgiveness of sins, in the beginning of the gospel about Jesus Christ, the Son of God, the saving Messiah.

The baptism with the Holy Spirit

In Mark we also see a *contrast* between John and Jesus. This also points forward to a saving Messiah: 'And this was his message: "After me will come one more powerful than I, the thongs of whose sandals I am not worthy to stoop down and untie. I baptize you with water, but he will baptize you with the Holy Spirit" ' (Mark 1:7).

Both Matthew and Luke mention this, adding the words 'and with fire' after 'Holy Spirit', and going on to expound the theme of judgement with imagery taken from the harvest scene. The Messiah sifts the wheat, stores the grain and burns the chaff (Matt. 3:11-12; Luke 3:16-17). Mark's emphasis here is to stress the Messiah's positive work. He brings the covenant blessing of the gift of the Holy Spirit. Mark's brief assertion about the Spirit, together with his selection of limited detail about John, serve to point out the contrast between Jesus and John. We see the beginning of the gospel about Jesus Christ both in the ministry of John and in the arrival of Jesus. So he presses on with this theme, first marking the striking similarity and then the contrast between the two.

Mark contrasts the ministries of John and the Lord Jesus: John baptizes with water; Jesus baptizes with the Holy Spirit. What does it mean when John says, 'He will baptize you with the Holy Spirit'? Historically, of course, this was fulfilled on the Day of Pentecost (Acts 1:5; 2:1-4). Subsequently, we see baptism with the Holy Spirit taking place at critical junctures during the spread of the gospel message to the Jews (Acts 1:8), to the Samaritans (Acts 8:15-17), to the Gentiles (Acts 10:44-48) and to some incompletely instructed Ephesians (Acts 19:4-6).

Some see it as a 'second' work of grace after an initial coming to faith. First, they say, we accept Jesus as Saviour and are 'saved'; then, we submit to Jesus as Lord and are 'baptized with the Holy Spirit'. But surely this cannot be the meaning? Paul writes to Roman Christians, 'And if anyone does not have the Spirit of Christ, he does not belong to Christ' (Rom. 8:9). He writes to Corinthian Christians, 'For we were all baptized by one Spirit into one body — whether Jews or Greeks, slave or free — and we were all given the one Spirit to drink' (1 Cor. 12:12). So we cannot be Christians without the indwelling Holy Spirit. The feature which characterizes Christians of all nationalities and classes is that they are all 'baptized by one Spirit'. Indeed, it is only though the working of the Holy Spirit that a man believes in the Lord Jesus as Saviour.

Being baptized with the Holy Spirit is not a second work of grace, but *the* work of grace. It is the action whereby Jesus as Messiah saves his elect. God baptizes them with the Holy Spirit, making them his heirs by bringing them into obedience to himself and imputing to them the benefit of the righteousness of Christ in place of their unrighteousness. In the eyes of God, all believers are clothed in the perfect righteousness of the Saviour. Jesus, anointed with the Holy Spirit as Messiah, anoints us by baptizing us with the Holy Spirit when he saves us from our sin. This comes about in repentance for sin and faith in Jesus Christ. It is Jesus as Messiah who saves by his grace and his sovereign initiative.

John stresses the difference between superficial and real faith: 'But you have an anointing from the Holy One, and all of you know the truth' (1 John 2:20). 'I am writing these things to you about those who are trying to lead you astray. As for you, the anointing you received from him remains in you, and you do not need anyone to teach you. But as his anointing teaches you about all things and as that anointing is real, not counterfeit — just as it has taught you, remain in him' (1 John 2:26-27).

Paul makes the same point as he assures the Ephesian Christians of their salvation: 'Having believed, you were marked in him with a seal, the promised Holy Spirit, who is a deposit guaranteeing our inheritance until the redemption of those who are God's possession — to the praise of his glory' (Eph. 1:13-14).

Jesus the Messiah not only seeks but saves the lost. Mark explains this through Jesus' baptism. Anointed with the Spirit, Jesus anoints others with the Spirit. Baptized with the Spirit, he baptizes others with the Spirit. That is his work. To that end he was anointed as Messiah by God. The Messianic office of Christ is a saving work. Jesus saves by baptizing with the Holy Spirit.

A. A. Hoekema writes, 'Summing up once again, we have seen that the expression "to be baptized in the Spirit" is used in the Gospels and in Acts 1:5 to designate the once-for-all historical event of the outpouring of the Holy Spirit at Pentecost — an event which can never be repeated. In Acts 11:16 the expression describes the reception of the Spirit for salvation

by people who were not Christians before. In 1 Corinthians
12:13 the expression describes the sovereign act of God
whereby all Christians are incorporated into the body of Christ
at the time of regeneration. Never in the New Testament is the
expression "to be baptized in the Spirit" used to describe a
post-conversion reception of the totality or fulness of the
Spirit.'

Mark's contrast between Jesus and John anticipates all of
this. The one who baptizes with the Holy Spirit is obviously a
saving Messiah.

Mark's summary of the gospel

What an intriguing beginning to Mark's story! Jesus has not
even arrived on the scene. Yet Mark has said so much about
the beginning of the gospel. The triune God is there, Father,
Son and Holy Spirit originating, accomplishing, applying the
gospel. The authority of Scripture is there, predicting a fulfilled gospel. The person of Christ is there, Jesus the Son of
God bringing the gospel. The work of Christ is there, for the
Messiah will baptize with the Holy Spirit, as he confers the
benefits of the gospel. The heart of the gospel is there in em-
bryo, a baptism of 'repentance' for 'the forgiveness of sins'.
And Mark shows all this without a nativity story or genealogi-
cal list!

Had those disciples Paul met at Ephesus only had the first
few snippets of Mark's Gospel, they would certainly have
known more than they did, for they knew simply of John's
baptism and had never heard that there was a Holy Spirit (Acts
19:1-7). That is why we commend Mark's Gospel as begin-
ner's reading for the interested or newly converted. It is simple,
but not simplistic. It is just packed full of instruction about a
full, biblical salvation!

Sufficient

Mark's Messiah is a sufficient Messiah. Jesus brings a sense of total fulfilment to those whom he seeks and saves. He satisfies people with the salvation he brings. Delivering them from the slavery of sin, he introduces them to a new life of purpose and meaning. This comes about because of who he is and what he does. Mark stresses Jesus' person and work and shows the sufficiency of his saviourhood. He does so in a fast-moving sequence of significant events, one following the other in quick succession like rapid bursts of gunfire. Mark's Gospel is action-packed. Matthew majors on the teaching Jesus gave, Luke on the people Jesus met, but Mark on the things Jesus did. 'At once' is a frequent expression in Mark. He laces his short sentences together with 'and', while Matthew and Luke opt for a more flowing style. In Mark the rapid succession of events discloses a sufficient Messiah.

The baptism of Jesus

We see the Lord Jesus anointed by the Spirit with power and authority for the work ahead. Empowered by the Father, he baptizes with the Holy Spirit. Right at the outset of his ministry, his saving work bears the impress of the triune God: 'As Jesus was coming up out of the water, he saw heaven being torn open and the Spirit descending on him like a dove. And a voice came from heaven: "You are my Son, whom I love; with you I am well pleased" ' (Mark 1:10-11).

The voice at Jesus' baptism in all three Synoptic Gospels echoes Old Testament themes: 'You are my Son, whom I love; with you I am well pleased.' Jesus was God's beloved Son, to whom God had given the nations as an inheritance (Ps. 2:7-8). Jesus was also God's chosen servant, upon whom God had put his Spirit to bring justice to the nations (Isa. 42:1).

Mark's presentation emphasizes the sufficiency of Jesus' authority. His language is gripping. The heavens are 'torn' apart by the mighty power of God. The voice echoes with power in the chasm, while the Spirit, by contrast, glides gently like a dove upon the Son. The authority of judgement and the tenderness of love combine in Mark's description. The transcendent God is now immanent with his people. The deliverer has come gently to seek and mightily to save the lost. Mark's vivid language accentuates the sufficiency of Christ.

The temptation in the desert

From here, Mark takes us straight to the desert: 'At once the Spirit sent him out into the desert, and he was in the desert for forty days, being tempted by Satan. He was with the wild animals, and angels attended him' (Mark 1:12-13).

The second burst of gunfire erupts. There are no details of the temptations or of Jesus' verbal battle with the devil, as in Matthew and Luke. But this is more than compensated for by Mark's unique presentation. Jesus is 'sent', not just 'led', into the desert, for the test was both ordained by God and urgent (Mark 1:12; cf. Matt. 4:1; Luke 4:1). Jesus combats Satan, 'the adversary' seeking to obstruct his path. In Mark Jesus is not only comforted by angels but accompanied by 'wild animals' (Mark 1:13; cf. Matt. 4:11). Mark also gives the distinct impression that this test was open-ended. It continued throughout Jesus' ministry. He 'has been tempted in every way, just as we are — yet was without sin' (Heb. 4:15), so that in faithfulness he continues to help those who are tempted. What a word for the Christians at Rome, about to face trials and persecution! While Mark gives none of the content of the tests Jesus faced and says nothing about their relevance to his ministry, the summary description and the graphic horrific detail included in his account of the temptation stress the sufficiency of Christ's faithfulness in this startling episode.

The preaching of Jesus

In Mark, we see the Messiah preaching fulfilled prophecy and the necessity for salvation. ' "The time has come," he said. "The kingdom of God is near. Repent and believe the good news!" ' (Mark 1:15).

Repentance and faith are mentioned by Mark as the twin demands of the gospel, the beginning of which he is expounding. The nearness of the kingdom requires not only, negatively, repentance of sin but, positively, faith in Christ. Mark here says in his own emphatic way in the first few lines of his Gospel what Paul spent two and a half years explaining to the Ephesian elders: 'I have declared to both Jews and Greeks that they must turn to God in repentance and have faith in our Lord Jesus' (Acts 20:21).

The calling of the disciples

After this revelation of Jesus as the Messiah, we see the Lord Jesus choosing disciples and promising them God's help in life-transforming service. Jesus urges them to follow him. In that way, their whole lives will be changed: ' "Come, follow me," Jesus said, "and I will make you fishers of men" ' (Mark 1:17). This is the final burst of gunfire. The succession of events originating the gospel culminates in the calling of the disciples. What makes Mark's account so striking is its context. Immediately after Jesus' words about repentance and believing the gospel, Mark gives us two active illustrations of what this means: the calling of Simon and Andrew and that of James and John. To believe the gospel is to follow Christ, and to follow Christ is to abandon everything and obey him first and foremost. This meant for these men, in particular, and for all believers, in general, abandoning everything to follow Christ and finding a life-transforming change pulsating with the purpose of Christ. From being fishermen they would become fishers of men. The faith that is obedient is the result of a regeneration that is effective:

> Loved with everlasting love,
> Led by grace that love to know,
> Spirit breathing from above,
> Thou hast taught me it is so.
> Oh, this full and perfect peace!
> Oh, this transport all divine!
> In a love which cannot cease
> I am his and he is mine.
>
> Heaven above is softer blue,
> Earth around is sweeter green,
> Something lives in every hue
> Christless eyes have never seen;
> Birds with gladder songs o'erflow,
> Flowers with deeper beauties shine,
> Since I know as now I know
> I am his and he is mine.
>
> (George Wade Robinson)

What a remarkable beginning to the Gospel of Mark! The initiative of the triune God in this good news is evident: God the Father plans, God the Son accomplishes and God the Spirit applies the salvation which lies at the heart of the good news. Man is called to repentance and faith: a real repentance leading to complete forgiveness, an active faith resulting in obedient service. The order of salvation is expressed in language we can understand. Man does not produce this salvation; God does through the good news of his Son, Jesus the promised Messiah. God commands and draws men to the place of repentance and faith. All this emerges as Mark starts his story without either birth-account or line of generations. The beginning of the gospel of Jesus Christ, the Son of God, is summed up by Mark in a seeking, saving and sufficient Messiah.

The secrecy surrounding the identity of the Messiah

There is something else striking here. Of all the Gospel writers, it is Mark who most stresses the secrecy of Jesus as Messiah. Again and again, Mark notes how Jesus commanded those whom he healed not to disclose his identity as Messiah. He silenced demons and demanded the same secrecy of his disciples. It is only at the end that Jesus openly asserts that he is Messiah. Yet here at the beginning Mark reveals all and then continues his account veiled with a secrecy which adds excitement to the unfolding sequence of events. But the end is there at the very beginning, the revelation of who Messiah is.

We meet this Messiah in the conversion of every Christian. My friend had a harmful habit. He had been brought up in a Christian home and attended church, Sunday school, Youth Fellowship and Boys' Brigade. He knew the facts of the gospel from childhood. On occasions, he had chatted with me about becoming a Christian, and had even attempted to do so, but found it to be a flawed exercise. No vital change came about; nothing seemed to have happened. This situation repeated itself and I was afraid of frustration leading to antagonism. I tried as best I could to help, but to little avail.

Circumstances made things worse for him. Eventually, finding himself near to despair, he heard a guest-speaker at our church whose story was so similar to his own. God spoke forcefully to him on that occasion, bringing him to what I now recognize to have been true repentance and faith. The change was remarkable. Scripture became alive to him, prayer a vital part of his life. The sinful habit was, with great difficulty, finally laid to rest. Other problems were resolved. His wife, a Christian, testified to the change in his temperament and nature. Christ became a living reality to them in their married life.

It would have been easy to see a merely human explanation to that change: a determination to deal with the habit that he had not previously demonstrated; the collusion of circumstances which produced emotional trauma and eventually 'conversion to Christ'. But the more I talked to him, the more I realized that reformation was the result, not the source, of his spiritual change and the emotional trauma was spiritual rather than psychological.

Earlier in his pathway to faith, human reformation had been present as he sought Christ, but even then Christ was seeking him in order to bring about regeneration. The result of Christ's seeking was a true saving. The implication of Christ's sufficiency was a lasting satisfaction. Jesus Christ, the Son of God, had revealed himself to my friend as a seeking, saving and sufficient Messiah. That was the beginning of the gospel for him.

Mark focuses on Jesus, the Son of God, as Messiah. That is the beginning of the gospel. The predictions of the prophets, the proclamation of John the Baptist, the baptism, temptations and preaching of Jesus all point in that direction. Jesus is the Messiah who seeks, saves and satisfies his people. The plan of God in Old Testament prophecy anticipates this. The silence of prophecy between Malachi and John the Baptist heightens the sense of expectation. John's ministry leads naturally and inevitably to Jesus. The voice at Jesus' baptism confirms it all. His resisting of Satan's temptation vindicates it. The Lord Jesus Christ is where the gospel begins.

On Jordan's bank the Baptist's cry
Announces that the Lord is nigh;
Come, then, and hearken, for he brings
Glad tidings from the King of kings.

Then cleansed be every breast from sin;
Make straight the way for God within;
Prepare we in our hearts a home
Where such a mighty Guest may come.

For thou art our salvation, Lord,
Our refuge, and our great reward;
Without thy grace we waste away,
Like flowers that wither and decay.

To him who left the throne of heaven
To save mankind, all praise be given;
Like praise be to the Father done,
And Holy Spirit, Three in One.

(Charles Coffin trans. by John Chandler)

2.
Mysterious God-man

Mark clearly portrays Jesus as man. Everywhere in his Gospel Christ's humanity is seen. We are left with the impression of a real person walking the shores of Galilee or moving through the streets of Jerusalem. This is clear, above all, in Jesus' emotions: anger, sorrow, surprise, disappointment, sympathy are all there in a full-blooded human picture of the Saviour. Yet throughout the Gospel Jesus is also portrayed as more than just a man.

We see this at the beginning of Mark. A man with leprosy comes to Jesus and begs to be healed: 'Filled with compassion, Jesus reached out his hand and touched the man' (Mark 1:41). This is dramatic. Jesus is so moved with pity that he touches the untouchable. Mark only, as compared with Matthew and Luke, mentions Jesus' emotion of compassion. Whatever degree of sympathy the sight of the wretch might evoke, the risk of infection would prevent the most human of ordinary men and women from actually touching the man. To see photographs or slides of compassionate people working to relieve lepers is to feel admiration for those who do such a work, but revulsion at the sight of mutilated limbs and deformed faces. The idea of touching such pitiful folk becomes frightening and even intolerable. But Jesus did touch them. His compassion transcends fear. His is a true humanity, but it is humanity with a difference, for it carries with it the power of God to heal. In the leper, we see a picture of man's sinfulness. Here is a debilitating disease, one which separated the Israelite from 'holy things' in tabernacle or temple worship and resulted in his being placed 'outside the camp' (Lev. 13:45-46). So sinners are placed outside the kingdom of God until Christ, in compassion, heals them.

The same mysterious humanity shines through at the end of the Gospel account. Mark's account of Jesus' experience in Gethsemane is different from those of Matthew and Luke and is peculiarly his own. The language Mark uses and the effect it conveys is unique. While Matthew uses the usual Greek term (*'lupeisthai'*) to describe Jesus' sorrowful distress, Mark employs a stronger expression (*'ekthambeisthai'*), 'deeply distressed', to convey Jesus' feelings. The term implies sorrow and fear. 'He took Peter, James and John along with him, and he began to be deeply distressed and troubled. "My soul is overwhelmed with sorrow to the point of death," he said to them. "Stay here and keep watch"' (Mark 14:33-34).

This was traumatic. The sense of increasing fear at the prospect of death for the sin of his people and the desire to have companions within earshot in his distress are all so human. We would expect such emotions of ourselves. We are amazed at them in Jesus.

John Murray says, 'Mark tells us that "he began to be amazed" (14:33). The inference is inevitable. There now invaded his consciousness such increased understanding and experience of the involvements of his commitment, that amazement filled his soul. Our Lord was now looking into the abyss that he was to swallow up in himself. The recoil of his whole soul was inevitable. If he had not recoiled from the incomparable ordeal, it would be unnatural in the deepest sense. We must reckon with the enormity of his agony and the reality of his human nature. Here was the unrelieved, unmitigated

judgement of God against sin. It filled him with horror and
dread. The recoil evidenced in the prayer is proof of the ordeal and of the necessary sensibilities and sensitivities of his
human nature.'

What is the reason for this startling picture of the humanity
of Jesus? What is the difference between his human nature
and ours? What is Mark saying to us in this portrayal? He is
showing us Jesus as the God-man. He is presenting to us the
portrait of a real man, yet one who is obviously much more
than a man. He is challenging us with the glory of the divine
and human natures of the person of Christ. The Son of God is
not only Messiah; he is God-man too. He is the Christ, the
Son of the living God. As B. B. Warfield puts it, 'Mark lays
particular stress on the Divine power of the human Jesus, as
evidence of his supernatural being; and on the irresistible impression of a veritable Son of God, a Divine being walking on
the earth as a man, which He made upon those with whom He
came into contact.'

New teaching

Mark discloses Jesus as God-man in the most natural of ways.
After the stirring beginning to his story, he gives us a typical
day in the life of Jesus. The view moves through the broad
sweep of Malachi's prophecy, the rough voice of John the
Baptist, the descent of the Holy Spirit on Jesus and the tur-
moil of temptation in the desert to a quiet country synagogue
in lakeside Capernaum on the Sabbath day.

The man who called Simon and Andrew, James and John
from their fishing to follow him goes with them to the synagogue in Capernaum. He begins to teach and immediately
causes baffled amazement: 'They went to Capernaum, and
when the Sabbath came, Jesus went into the synagogue and

began to teach. The people were amazed at his teaching, because he taught them as one who had authority, not as the teachers of the law' (Mark 1:21-22). 'The people were all so amazed that they asked each other, "What is this? A new teaching — and with authority! He even gives orders to evil spirits and they obey him" ' (Mark 1:27).

I remember at university that we used to discuss our lecturers. We were reading history and I suppose what we wanted most was a teacher who could rescue us from endless dates and events, give us an overview, a pattern, and inspire us to see the important details among the insignificant, to show us the wood amid the trees. Some did this well and we benefited from them, following the thread of their reasoning, interested to hear their interpretation. Listening to Jesus was listening to the greatest teacher who ever lived — his mastery of detail, his eye for the significant, his depth of perception.

Jesus' teaching was unlike that of the scribes and Pharisees. They quoted their authorities, compiled their Mishnah, or law-book, developed the rules of their Halakah, or 'instructions for the walk of life', and commented on the Scriptures. Often their words were more harmful than helpful: unnecessary additions, flawed omissions, basic misconceptions. Regulations became pernickety. They strained at gnats but swallowed camels. They missed the point. Tithes of anise, mint and cummin took the place of justice, mercy and faithfulness. They substituted the traditions of men for the Word of God. Jesus was not like that.

His authority

It was not just that Jesus was a good communicator, or an expert in picking out what was significant in the Torah. There was more to it than that. Jesus did not rely on the traditions of men. When he spoke, it was as though God spoke. He identified

with God and Scripture in a way that was unique, for he himself is Scripture's author. Had the teachers of the law done
this, it would have been blasphemous.

We see Jesus' authority once more in the story of the demoniac who interrupted the synagogue service in Capernaum:
' "What do you want with us, Jesus of Nazareth? Have you
come to destroy us? I know who you are — the Holy One of
God!" "Be quiet!" said Jesus sternly. "Come out of him!" The
evil spirit shook the man violently and came out of him with a
shriek' (Mark 1:24-25).

The words of the demon-possessed man must have amazed
his hearers too: Jesus of Nazareth — the Holy One of God? A
man who could not only teach as he did but command evil
spirits was certainly to be heeded. This was a new teaching,
with the authority of exorcising demons in his own name to
confirm it.

The reaction of his hearers

Sadly, while the people were attentive to his teaching, they
showed little sign of being convinced. They admired the teacher,
but not to the point of following him. Mark pursues this reaction in his story. Indeed, this is a recurring theme throughout the remainder of Mark's Gospel. The events of that typical day in Capernaum were representative of his whole ministry.
Mark is showing us the mysterious God-man, not only in the
unique things Jesus taught and did, but also in the reaction of
the people to those things. The mystery of Jesus constantly
causes wonder and astonishment in this Gospel.

Later in Mark there is another striking reference to this
reaction to Jesus' teaching. Jesus visits his own synagogue at
Nazareth and begins to teach on the Sabbath. The effect is
similar: 'When the Sabbath came, he began to teach in the

synagogue, and many who heard him were amazed' (Mark 6:1-2).

This time, however, the amazement had a critical flavour. Where did this man get these things — this wisdom, this miraculous power? 'Isn't this the carpenter? Isn't this Mary's son and the brother of James, Joseph, Judas and Simon? Aren't his sisters here with us?' (Mark 6:3). They took offence, and to such an extent that Jesus curtailed his ministry there — he performed no miracles apart from a few healings. They were amazed, but then, Jesus was amazed at them, too: 'And he was amazed at their lack of faith' (Mark 6:6).

Mark's portrayal of this reaction to Jesus' teaching is pronounced. Through it again we can see Jesus the mysterious God-man clearly. Luke describes a similar reaction earlier in his story, on the occasion of Jesus' visit to his home synagogue in Nazareth (Luke 4:16-30). Luke closes his account of this by showing the anger of Jesus' fellow-villagers, who were about to throw him off a hill to his death. Mark's presentation adds further details to sharpen the focus on the mystery of who Jesus is. Jesus is not just the carpenter's son, but a carpenter himself (Mark 6:3). The wisdom Jesus reveals has been given to him in particular (Mark 6:2). The miracles are the work of Jesus' own hands (Mark 6:2). In this way, Mark stresses the amazement of the people at Jesus' words and deeds. Mark, alone of the evangelists, notes Jesus' reaction to their unbelief: 'And he was amazed at their lack of faith' (Mark 6:6). That the all-knowing God, in human nature, should experience amazement is indeed a mystery to us. Yet, what comfort we gain from it, as we in turn are amazed at the unbelief of the world around us!

Awe and wonder do not guarantee discipleship. Amazement at the teacher, even awareness of his divinity, does not necessarily express true conversion. Attentiveness to the true and challenging nature of Christ's words can lead to the brink of faith without resulting in faith. The lawyer whom Jesus commended for being near the kingdom of God may have left the matter there. Felix trembled as he listened to Paul, but we never read of his conversion to Christ. Attention to Christ's teaching is not enough. It must lead on to faith in him, if it is to accomplish its purpose. 'That the Word may become effectual to salvation, we must attend thereunto with diligence, preparation and prayer; receive it with faith and love, lay it up in our hearts, and practise it in our lives' (*Shorter Catechism,* 90).

We see this particularly in those who, having been brought up in a Christian family, sit under the ministry of the gospel week after week, without any manifestation of saving faith. Familiarity can so easily breed contempt and, if the often-heard word of the gospel is not mixed with faith, it can harden.

The amazed did not inevitably become Christ's followers. Just prior to Peter's confession at Caesarea Philippi, Mark notes the effect of Jesus' healing power on a deaf-and-dumb man (Mark 7:32-37). Jesus puts his fingers in the man's ears as though to unplug them, spits and, with his saliva, appears to lubricate the man's tongue. Then he breathes out, saying 'Ephaththa! — Be opened!', as if to ventilate the man's hearing and speech with his own breath. Healing is immediate. The man, who had previously made garbled sounds, now speaks clearly. The effect on the crowd is electrifying: 'People were overwhelmed with amazement. "He has done everything well," they said. "He even makes the deaf hear and the mute speak" ' (Mark 7:37).

This is remarkable. There are no parallel accounts in either Matthew or Luke of this healing of the deaf-and-dumb man. It bears all the characteristics of Mark's style, being full of action. It focuses on Jesus' humanity during the healing. We can see it all happening. Like a journalist, Mark gives the minimum of detail, isolates salient features and gets the message across vividly. We gaze in wonder at Jesus as he puts his fingers into the man's ears, spits, touches the man's tongue and breathes on the man, using his body as the means of healing him. The man is healed miraculously. The divine and human meet in Jesus and cause the cure.

We see in this healing a picture of conversion, for we are all deaf to every utterance of God's Word, and dumb to speak his praise. Our ears must be unstopped and our tongues untied. God could have healed the deaf-and-dumb man with a single word, but he chose to use 'means'. So it is with man: the triune God enacts the greatest miracle of all, salvation of the soul, though the simplest of means, the 'foolishness of [the message] preached' (1 Cor. 1:21).

Christ then commands silence, as he so often does, but to no avail. Mark notes, as he has done already, the astonished reaction of the crowd. Now they applaud rather than criticize. The narrative fits into Mark's scheme of things. We see Jesus the mysterious God-man at work. There is, truly, with Jesus the irresistible impression of 'a veritable son of God, a Divine being walking on the earth as a man, which He made upon those with whom He came into contact' (B. B. Warfield).

That astonished reaction, however, did not mean that the people accepted Jesus' mastery and became his disciples. To be filled with astonishment, awe and even praise for Jesus, as a miracle-worker, did not constitute saving faith. It may be a part of true faith, or may eventually lead to it, but we must not make the mistake of thinking that wonderment means salvation. Too often people are romantically caught up with the person of Christ, yet it does not produce lasting commitment to his claims. In this incident Mark is warning against the danger of superficial excitement about Jesus' person and power leading to spurious discipleship.

New healing

From the synagogue in Capernaum, Jesus and his disciples go
to Simon's home. Simon's mother-in-law is in bed with a fe-
ver. They tell Jesus and he heals her. The cure is so immediate
that she gets up there and then to serve them. The news spreads
like wildfire. That evening the home is packed with the sick
and demon-possessed and Jesus continues his healing ministry
among them. Henry Twells catches the atmosphere of that
occasion in his hymn relating the variety of illnesses, the power
of spiritual as well as physical healing, the humanity and divinity of Jesus:

> At even when the sun was set,
> The sick, O Lord, around thee lay;
> Oh, in what divers pains they met!
> Oh, with what joy they went away!
>
> O Saviour Christ, our woes dispel:
> For some are sick, and some are sad,
> And some have never loved thee well,
> And some have lost the love they had.
>
> And some are pressed with worldly care,
> And some are tried with sinful doubt;
> And some such grievous passions tear
> That only thou canst cast them out.
>
> O Saviour Christ, thou too art Man;
> Thou hast been troubled, tempted, tried;
> Thy kind but searching glance can scan
> The very wounds that shame would hide;

Thy touch has still its ancient power;
No word from thee can fruitless fall:
Hear in this solemn evening hour,
And in thy mercy heal us all.

His authority over evil spirits

Mark stresses the variety of afflictions that Jesus heals. Chief among them is demon-possession. The demon-possessed are healed and the demons commanded to be silent, for they know who Jesus is (Mark 1:32-34). Religious men and quack healers cured the ordinary round of diseases but not demon-possession. This stands apart even from psychosomatic disorders. It is not just a nervous or mental disturbance; it is a much more sinister condition than that.

J. S. Wright says, 'Apparent possession by spirits is a world-wide phenomenon. It may be sought deliberately, as by shaman and witch-doctor among primitive peoples, and by the medium among both primitive and civilized men and women. It may come upon individuals suddenly, as with watchers at the Voodoo rites, or in the form of what is generally known as demon-possession. In each case the possessed person behaves in a way that is not normal for him or her, speaks in a voice totally different from normal, and often shows power of telepathy and clairvoyance ... it should be noted that the Bible never speaks of possession by any good departed spirit or by an angel. The alternatives are either the Holy Spirit or an evil spirit.'

Jesus' power to exorcise evil spirits showed his total supremacy in the spirit world. This was a new kind of healing. This set the seal on his new teaching (Mark 1:27). Coupled with his preaching in the synagogues, it was a marked characteristic of his ministry: 'So he travelled throughout Galilee, preaching in their synagogues and driving out demons' (Mark 1:39).

Mark's emphases again stand out distinctly. For him these events are 'immediate' in their succession — a characteristic expression of his. The new teaching is followed by new healing — immediately (see Mark 1:23,28,29).

'The whole town gathered at the door, and Jesus healed many who had various diseases. He also drove out demons, but he would not let the demons speak because they knew who he was' (Mark 1:34). Mark wants us to recognize the mysterious authority of Jesus the God-man in his healing, not simply of various disorders, but of demon-possession. Neither the disciples nor the crowd recognize the true identity of Jesus, but the demons do. Christ the Messiah does not only reign over the material world, but is Lord over all 'the rulers ... the authorities ... the powers of this dark world and ... the spiritual forces of evil in the heavenly realms' (Eph. 6:12). He saves his people from their sin.

New priorities

Prayer

The story turns from a day in the life of Jesus to events occurring the next morning. Crowds appear at Peter's door but Jesus is not to be found. Where can he be? Mark explains Jesus' absence in simple, unforgettable language: 'Very early in the morning, while it was still dark, Jesus got up, left the house and went off to a solitary place, where he prayed' (Mark 1:35).

That was remarkable — not that he should rise in the dark before dawn, for sleeplessness can come to all mankind; nor that he should seek solitude, but that Jesus, the God-man, should pray! When we lose a sense of amazement at that, we miss Mark's purpose that we should consider carefully who Jesus is. We read other accounts of Jesus' prayer life, including a whole night spent in prayer before he chose his disciples. We read of the tearing agony of Gethsemane. We listen with wonder to Jesus' words to his Father in John 17. Mark here forces us back to basics, to consider this alone: Jesus prays.

How much we learn of Jesus from this! His divine love draws him to talk to his Father in prayer, expressing the intimacy in glory that they shared before the world began. The eternal Son converses with the eternal Father. His human nature remarkably drives him to seek his Father. Exhausted in body and mind, amazed that they would want him as a healer but ignore him as Saviour, God the Son seeks comfort and prays for more resources from his heavenly Father. If we are to take Jesus' human nature seriously, then surely we should dwell on the fact that love and need moved Jesus to pray.

There is so much we must learn here about the priority of prayer. I scan the poverty of my own experience of prayer down the years. I recall the early days of faith, a prayer meeting at seven o'clock on Saturday morning and half-past eight on Sunday morning — the rich rewards for the slight sacrifice involved. I reflect on the 'quiet time' of a working student, fitting prayer into the day's routine. I contemplate the practical difficulties for the working man trying to do the same. But I remember, above all, my frequent apathy, forgetfulness, neglect and familiarity with a routine that breeds contempt. I think of the many praying folk in my congregation, the retired people, their prayer lists, their answers to prayer and their faithfulness to the prayer meeting. I recall the discouragement of inviting so many to come to the prayer meeting and yet, at times, seeing so few. Here in Mark we see Jesus alone, early in the morning, praying.

Surely the priority of prayer must grip us again as we consider its importance for Christ. Christ's practice of prayer calls us anew to talk with our heavenly Father, to bring everything to him in prayer, to engage in this as a warm, refreshing activity rather than a cold, formal routine. Jesus teaches the need for this new priority to sweep over and control our life.

Sweet hour of prayer, sweet hour of prayer,
That calls me from a world of care,
And bids me at my Father's throne
Make all my wants and wishes known;
In seasons of distress and grief
My soul has often found relief,
And oft escaped the tempter's snare
By thy return, sweet hour of prayer.

                                          (W. W. Walford)

The preaching of the Word

The other priority which is highlighted here is listening to the Word. Peter and his friends must have been so surprised when, having eventually found Jesus, they listened to his response to their announcement that 'Everyone is looking for you!' (Mark 1:37). 'Jesus replied, "Let us go somewhere else — to the nearby villages — so that I can preach there also. That is why I have come" ' (Mark 1:38).

That Jesus should seek solitude after the rush of the previous day would have been understandable. That he should intend moving elsewhere was probably incredible to the disciples. He had shown compassion to Peter's family. He had extended that care to a number of the townsfolk. His fame was on the crest of the wave after just one Sabbath day's ministry there. To abandon the area and move to another place at that juncture must have seemed like lunacy to them. People were crowding outside Peter's door at that very moment because of Jesus. For Jesus to leave now was hardly furthering his popularity and his cause.

But Jesus did move and gave his reason for doing so. His *raison d'être*, the essence of his ministry, the passion behind his actions, was to *preach*, not to heal. He had the message of a kingdom to announce and good news of deliverance to tell. There were men and women to save from sin. This was his priority: 'So he travelled throughout Galilee, preaching in their synagogues and driving out demons' (Mark 1:39).

Twinned priorities

Mark, therefore, stresses prayer and the preaching of the Word as twinned priorities; the latter confirmed not just generally by healing miracles but specifically by exorcisms. These priorities are constantly stressed throughout the New Testament as of fundamental importance (Acts 6:4; 1 Thess. 5:17; 2 Tim. 4:2; James 5:20; 1 Peter 4:7-11). Preaching the Word, proclaiming the good news of the kingdom of God, must always have top priority in the church's agenda. The apostles turned from important financial administrative duties to concentrate on the even more important matters of prayer and the Word (Acts 6:5). These go hand-in-hand. They are twinned priorities. How sad to hear a churchman say, in a recent television documentary about the work of the Christian ministry as we enter the twenty-first century, that he was 'not in business to see people converted, but simply to say that the church was there'! The documentary followed a typical day in his life's work, but he appeared as an irrelevant, ill-respected visitor, making some kind of a point that people were not particularly interested in. How different the intense passion of Jesus the

God-man, laying emphasis on the care of others, showing true concern for the creature where it is most required, but above all meeting in his redeeming grace the real need of men's souls! Jesus gets on with the work of the kingdom. May we ever follow his example!

The response of the disciples

At this point, Mark begins to focus on the response of the disciples, rather than that of the crowd. Attention to Jesus' teaching did not inevitably produce conviction of its truth and discipleship. Amazement at his healing miracles did not invariably result in conversion to his cause. Even among his disciples, education through the miraculous did not yield full enlightenment. Unable to come to terms with the God-man's power, his followers still did not understand.

We see the disciples witnessing Jesus' healing of a paralysed man a few days later in Capernaum (Mark 2:1-11). Jesus surprises the company with the pronouncement: 'Son, your sins are forgiven' (Mark 2:5), alternated with the command: 'Get up, take your mat and walk' (Mark 2:9). To forgive sins and to heal the body with a word are both equally easy for Jesus. The teachers of the law fumed, everyone was amazed, but did the disciples really understand? 'He got up, took his mat and walked out in full view of them all. This amazed everyone and they praised God, saying, "We have never seen anything like this!" ' (Mark 2:12).

Later, having miraculously fed more than five thousand people, Jesus walked across the water to the boat. The disciples were petrified and mystified, but still not enlightened: 'Then he climbed into the boat with them, and the wind died down. They were completely amazed, for they had not understood about the loaves; their hearts were hardened' (Mark 6:51-52).

They had opportunity, too, to review the matter, after Jesus worked another miracle, this time with four loaves (Mark 8:14-21), but even then true understanding was not theirs. On this occasion the disciples took refuge from the crowd in a boat. They had forgotten to bring bread for themselves. Jesus warned them: 'Be careful... Watch out for the yeast of the Pharisees and that of Herod' (Mark 8:15). They thought Jesus was angry with them for forgetting bread.

Jesus challenges their continuing hardness of heart:

Aware of their discussion, Jesus asked them: 'Why are you talking about having no bread? Do you still not see or understand? Are your hearts hardened? Do you have eyes but fail to see, and ears but fail to hear? And don't you remember? When I broke the five loaves for the five thousand, how many basketfuls of pieces did you pick up?'

'Twelve,' they replied.

'And when I broke the seven loaves for the four thousand, how many basketfuls of pieces did you pick up?'

They answered, 'Seven.'

He said to them, 'Do you still not understand?' (Mark 8:17-21).

Mark explores this uncomprehending reaction of the disciples to Jesus in his own unique way. Matthew, Mark and Luke all note the amazement of the crowd at Jesus, when he healed the paralysed man (Matt. 9:8; Mark 2:12; Luke 5:26). Luke does not mention Jesus walking on the water, nor the reaction to the feeding of the crowd. Matthew does and records a positive reaction from the disciples in the boat as the wind ceased.

Those in the boat claim that Jesus is truly the Son of God (Matt. 14:33). Mark, however, notes a mixed response from the disciples, as we have already seen (Mark 6:51-52).

Matthew also explains their reaction as a lack of faith, a failure in understanding, which could only be rectified as the disciples reflected on Jesus' warning about the leaven of the scribes and Pharisees (Matt. 16:5-12). Mark sees in that reaction not only a lack of understanding but, as Jesus' questions suggest again, hardness of heart. The problem is not just confusion of mind but stubbornness of will. Mark adds, 'Aware of their discussion, Jesus asked them: "Why are you talking about having no bread? Do you still not see or understand? Are your hearts hardened?" ' (Mark 8:17).

Then, Mark, alone of the evangelists, goes on to record the healing of the blind man of Bethsaida (Mark 8:22-26). The account recalls Mark's earlier story of the healing of the deaf-and-dumb man (Mark 7:32-37). There is the same vivid description, the emphasis on the actions of the human Jesus, here spitting on the eyes and putting his hands on the blind man. But, in this case, Mark describes the blind man as coming half-way to sight, seeing people like trees walking around. When Jesus then puts his hands on the man's eyes, he is completely restored and sees everything clearly (Mark 8:22-25). Immediately after this comes Peter's confession of faith at Caesarea Philippi (Matt. 16:13-20; Mark 8:27-30; Luke 9:18-21).

What is Mark saying to us here in specifying the disciples' dull reaction to the feeding of the crowd, in recording the healing of the blind man and then in following it with Peter's confession of Christ? He is surely stressing that the disciples do not see clearly who Jesus really is. Like the blind man, they see people walking like trees. Their minds are confused, for their hearts are hardened. There is growing evidence to convince their intellects, but their wills remain stubborn. They are on the road to grasping who Jesus really is, but they resist the implications of his claims. Jesus, the mysterious God-man, has amazed them, as he has the crowd.

The *Shorter Catechism* explains this: 'Effectual calling is the work of God's Spirit, whereby, convincing us of our sin and misery, enlightening our minds in the knowledge of Christ, and renewing our wills, he doth persuade and enable us to embrace Jesus Christ, freely offered to us in the Gospel' (*Shorter Catechism*, 31).

Mark, through the reactions of the crowd and the disciples to Jesus and in his portrayal of Jesus, shows that Jesus, the man from Nazareth, is at the same time the eternal Son of God.

Mrs C. H. Morris' words recall so well Jesus and his mysterious power in her poem, 'The Stranger of Galilee':

In fancy I stood by the shore one day,
Of the beautiful murmuring sea;
I saw the great crowds as they thronged the way
Of the Stranger of Galilee:
I saw how the man who was blind from birth
In a moment was made to see;
The lame was made whole by the matchless skill
Of the Stranger of Galilee.

His look of compassion,
His words of love,
They shall never forgotten be.
When sin-sick and helpless he saw me there,
This Stranger of Galilee;
He showed me his hand and his riven side,
And he whispered, 'It was for thee!'
My burden fell off at the pierced feet
Of the Stranger of Galilee.

I heard him speak peace to the angry waves,
Of that turbulent raging sea;
And lo! at his word are the waters stilled,
This Stranger of Galilee;
A peaceful, a quiet and holy calm,
Now and ever abides with me;
He holdeth my life in his mighty hands,
This Stranger of Galilee.

Come ye, who are driven, and tempest-tossed,
And his gracious salvation see;
He'll quiet life's storms with his 'Peace, be still!'
This Stranger of Galilee;
He bids me to go and the story tell
What he ever to you will be,
If only you let him with you abide,
This Stranger of Galilee.

And I felt I could love him for ever.
So gracious and tender was he!
I claimed him that day as my Saviour,
This Stranger of Galilee.

3.
Dynamic Prophet

Mark depicts Jesus as a prophet, indeed, the great Prophet to come. Prophets were God's vehicles of revelation in Old Testament days. People today often think of them as eccentric individuals or religious fanatics, extreme in their views and outspoken in their demands. But they were men set apart by God to speak in his name. Sometimes they went into a trance-like state as they delivered their oracles. Always they brought a message from God — 'the Word of the Lord'. Frequently they would do this in two ways: *foretelling* future events and *forth-telling,* or interpreting God's purpose in the present. God promised a Messiah who would be a prophet, a spokesman of God like Moses: 'The LORD your God will raise up for you a prophet like me from among your own brothers. You must listen to him' (Deut. 18:15).

The Lord Jesus spoke in parables. What are 'parables' and what connection do they have with the Old Testament prophets? I well remember learning as a boy in school the description of a parable as 'an earthly story with a heavenly meaning'. That is a description that has stood the test of time. We were also taught to distinguish between parable and allegory, between the method of teaching in the parable of the sower (Mark 4:1-20) and that in the Lord's description of himself as the vine (John 15:1-17), where he uses allegory. In the former

there is one key theme; in the latter each aspect of the earthly
story has a direct heavenly counterpart. The word 'parable'
has at its roots the meaning: 'to set two things alongside' —
the earthly story and the heavenly meaning. The spiritual moral
has a challenge in it, meant to arrest the hearer with a short,
sharp lesson.

The Old Testament prophets also used parables as stories,
riddles and proverbs. Whether story, riddle or proverb, the
purpose was always to bring the Word of God to the mind of
man in his earthly setting. Mark portrays Jesus as prophet using this method to perfection. By this means he arrests the
attention and brings God's Word to man's situation with unmistakable meaning.

Mark focuses on a unique aspect of Jesus' teaching as
prophet, which forcefully challenged people as they listened
in the most human of settings. Mark portrays Jesus as teaching primarily in parables: 'He taught them many things by parables' (Mark 4:2). 'He did not say anything to them without
using a parable' (Mark 4:34).

Of course, the other Gospel writers do the same. Indeed,
Matthew includes many more parables than Mark. Luke notes
their importance, while John selects for his readers allegories
more than parables. But, in Mark's own way, the forcefulness
of this side of Jesus' ministry comes through and stresses the
prophetic nature of his teaching.

Mark's distinctive note is intriguing. Matthew lists a number
of parables as examples of Jesus' teaching about the kingdom
(Matt. 13:1-53). This passage forms the first of five main blocks
of Jesus' teaching in his Gospel, in which the characteristic
note of fulfilment of Old Testament prophecy recurs. Luke
records the least number of parables (Luke 8:4-18) and shows
his particular interest in people: for example, in the accounts
of Jesus being anointed by a sinful woman and Jesus' contacts
with his mother and brothers (Luke 7:36-50; 8:19-21).

In Mark the teaching on parables comes early in the time sequence and forms the largest unit of Jesus' teaching in the Gospel (Mark 4:1-33). Mark's keynote is the *purpose* of this teaching. He is not content to give a few examples of this instruction, or simply to note its importance in passing, but majors on the reason for it and the motivation behind it. Mark is showing us the dynamism of Jesus the Prophet, as the Lord unlocks the mystery of the kingdom and interprets the riddle of the gospel. While Mark's account is simple, it is by no means simplistic. Deep theological truths about Jesus' prophetic mission as Messiah, disclosing the secret of the kingdom, are present here. The wonder of the mysterious God-man continues in Jesus the dynamic Prophet. The mystery and dynamism are both in Jesus' person and teaching.

William L. Lane says of Mark's unique approach: 'It is not Mark's intention to present an exhaustive account of Jesus' parabolic teaching, but to illustrate its form and content. Each of the three [parables] reflects upon sowing, growth and harvest — elements which illumine the character of the Kingdom of God. Mark appears to have selected these parables and placed them at this point in his presentation to illustrate the character of the coming of the Kingdom of God proclaimed by Jesus. They indicate that the presence of Jesus signals the release of the mysterious forces of God, which must culminate in the consummation and recognition of the majesty and sovereignty of God.'

Mark also stresses the *context* of Jesus' teaching in parables. Mark's section on parables stands amid chapters 3:7 - 6:6 and is followed by three accounts of Jesus' power. This context underwrites the authority of Jesus the prophet. The three incidents are the calming of the storm, the exorcism of a demon-possessed man and the restoration to wholeness of a dead girl and a sick woman. Mark specifies that it was on the evening of the day when Jesus explained the parables that he did these things: 'That day when evening came, he said to his disciples, "Let us go over to the other side" ' (Mark 4:35).

Both purpose and context speak of the mysterious sovereignty of Jesus the dynamic Prophet.

The message — the kingdom of God

Mark discloses that the message of Jesus' parables is primarily about the kingdom of God. He stresses, in particular, the sovereignty of God in the revelation of this kingdom. This is the thrust of Jesus' teaching as recorded in Mark 4:1-34. Through parables, Jesus teaches the secret of the kingdom of God (vv. 2,11,26,30).

Germination

Germination of the seed symbolizes the radical in-breaking of the kingdom of God into someone's life. The parable of the sower is really about the soils, as well as the seed. The reign of God in the life of man must have a definite and positive beginning. Initiation into the kingdom is neither accidental nor casual but studied and precise. Once there was no life; then life occurred. Once there were only potential and anticipation, but now reality and fulfilment. Germination must precede growth. A man must be born again. Except we turn and become as children, entry to the kingdom is barred. Germination is where God's kingdom begins.

Hindrances to germination abound:

The life-giving start can be *inhibited*: 'As he was scattering the seed, some fell along the path, and the birds came and ate it up' (Mark 4:4).

It can be *superficial*: 'Some fell on rocky places, where it did not have much soil. It sprang up quickly, because the soil was shallow. But when the sun came up, the plants were scorched, and they withered because they had no root' (Mark 4:5-6).

It may be *stunted*: 'Other seed fell among thorns, which grew up and choked the plants, so that they did not bear grain' (Mark 4:7).

Or it may be *successful*: 'Still other seed fell on good soil. It came up, grew and produced a crop, multiplying thirty, sixty, or even a hundred times' (Mark 4:8).

Whatever the obstacles, germination is necessary. Without it, the kingdom does not begin.

Growth

Growth marks the progression and development of the kingdom of God. The last of the soils makes this clear. The same is true of the other parables of Jesus recorded by Mark, those of the growing seed and the mustard seed.

The growth of the former is secret, divinely inspired, not humanly contrived: 'Night and day, whether he sleeps or gets up, the seed sprouts and grows, though he does not know how. All by itself the soil produces corn' (Mark 4:27-28).

The growth of the latter is spreading, divinely ordered, not humanly controlled: 'It is like a mustard seed, which is the smallest seed you plant in the ground. Yet when planted, it grows and becomes the largest of all garden plants, with such big branches that the birds of the air can perch in its shade' (Mark 4:31-32).

Growth is the natural outcome of germination, proof that germination has taken place. Jesus elsewhere recalls that by their fruits the children of the kingdom are known (Matt. 7:20). Disciples prove to be disciples as they remain in the vine and bear fruit (John 15:8). Jesus resolves the riddle of the kingdom of God by teaching the necessity of germination and growth.

The purpose of the message

This much is common ground with Matthew and Luke. Mark is distinctive in exposing the *purpose* of God in this message. Matthew includes a quotation from Isaiah and suggests that the reason why Jesus teaches in parables is to unfold the mystery of the kingdom to his followers. At the same time, the resulting effect on outsiders is to leave them confused in their minds and hardened in their wills:

> You will be ever hearing but never understanding;
>   you will be ever seeing but never perceiving.
> For this people's heart has become calloused;
>   they hardly hear with their ears,
>   and they have closed their eyes.
> Otherwise they might see with their eyes,
>   hear with their ears,
>   understand with their hearts
> and turn, and I would heal them
>   (Matt. 13:14-15; cf. Isa. 6:9-10).

Luke simply notes that Jesus communicates with his followers through parables and that this method presents a barrier for the outsider (Luke 8:9-10). While Matthew gives the distinct impression that the *result* of the parables in the life of the outsider is unbelief, Mark shows that it is the *purpose* of the parables to produce this effect in unbelievers:

When he was alone, the Twelve and the others around him asked him about the parables. He told them, 'The secret of the kingdom of God has been given to you. But to those on the outside everything is said in parables so that,

' "they may be ever seeing but never perceiving,
    and ever hearing but never understanding;
otherwise they might turn and be forgiven!" '

(Mark 4:10-12).

Surely Mark is not saying that God is vindictively confusing outsiders by their hearing of parables? By no means! What he is stressing is that God's purpose through Jesus' parables was, firstly, to clarify the meaning of the kingdom to the believer and, secondly, to expose the unbelief of the outsider with the simplicity of the message. Man must turn from his self-made solutions and find in Jesus alone the answer to his need. Parables sharpen the focus of the kingdom on Jesus the dynamic Prophet and produce either enlightened openness on the one hand, or stubborn resistance on the other. Mark underlines the truth that this mysterious and divisive process is within the sovereign purpose of God. The mystery of the kingdom is resolved in Jesus and in the forgiveness he alone bestows through repentance and faith. That is the purpose of the message of the parables, says Mark.

Endlessly in my ministry I return to the parable of the sower. It shows people what it means to come to faith and indicates the kind of instruction men need. It helps me understand why some do not come to faith, for the ground is hard, or stony, or weed-infested and needs to be broken up by prayer. It sets evangelism in a proper perspective, for salvation is not ultimately the work of man but of God. The parable of the sower drives us back to basics and resolves the riddles of diverse responses to human ministry again and again.

Far too often we rely upon human resources in God's work. Frustration and depression are the inevitable outcome. The problem is that we so often think of the work as *our* work, not *God's* work. We conveniently pay lip-service to divine sovereignty and then go about the work of the kingdom as though it only depended upon our efforts and expertise. But it does not, and if we follow that course of action, then depression and frustration are inevitable. Isaiah had to learn this lesson. God taught his prophet this so that he might not lose heart, but rather be encouraged in spite of the negative response of man. God would yet preserve his purpose in a remnant. The life was in the stump. God moves in mysterious ways, his wonders to perform. But it is God who moves. When we forget that we invite frustration and failure.

The method — a mystery disclosed

The parables reveal the mystery of the kingdom. Jesus discloses the secret of his rule as he explains the method of instruction. Why does Jesus go back to Isaiah the prophet for his explanation? Isaiah, enthusiastic in accepting God's call, is confronted by a most daunting prospect. God reminds him that his repeated efforts in prophesying to the people will prove fruitless. He will be like a person from a different country speaking a foreign language among them. The people will appear to respond, but it will be superficial. They will hear, but not understand; see, but not perceive. The more Isaiah preaches, the harder the people's hearts will become, their ears more dull, their eyes closed. 'How long?' asks Isaiah. God replies, 'Until cities are ruined, houses empty, the entire land ravaged.' Even what remains will be destroyed. Yet, like a felled tree, life will be in the stump. A remnant will yet hear and be saved.

Jesus quotes Isaiah to make two points. First, true response to the prophet's parables is something given by God, not earned. Second, ultimate success is nevertheless guaranteed by divine grace. Jesus stresses the 'given' nature of the disclosure of God's rule in man's life. It is a mystery presently unlocked, a secret now open, not to all and sundry, but only to those to whom God chooses to disclose it. This is not a matter of human intelligence, but of divine revelation; not of mental perception, but of enlightening grace.

Calvin writes in his *Harmony of the Gospels of Matthew, Mark and Luke*, 'To ascertain fully the meaning of the present passage, we must examine more closely the design of Christ, the reason why and the purpose for which these words were spoken. First, the comparison is undoubtedly intended by Christ to exhibit the magnitude of the grace bestowed upon his disciples, in having specially received what was not given indiscriminately to all. If it is asked why this privilege was peculiar to the disciples, the reason certainly will not be found in themselves; and Christ, by declaring that it was *given* to them excludes all merit. Christ declares that there are certain and elect men, on whom God specially bestows this honour of revealing to them his *secrets* and that others are deprived of his grace. No other reason will be found for this distinction, except that God calls to himself those whom he has gratuitously elected.'

The principle behind the parables

The principle underlying Mark's presentation of the parables is that salvation is all of grace, from start to finish. It is like God's message through Daniel to Nebuchadnezzar: 'No wise man, enchanter, magician or diviner can explain to the king the mystery he has asked about, but there is a God in heaven who reveals mysteries' (Dan. 2:27-28).

All three Gospel writers record Jesus' interpretation of the parables of the sower in detail. But, once again, Mark presents Jesus' explanation in his own special way. Matthew and Luke give Jesus' explanation as a *simple statement*: 'Listen then to what the parable of the sower means' (Matt. 13:18); 'This is the meaning of the parable' (Luke 8:11). Mark, however, records Jesus' words at that point as a *challenging question*: 'Then Jesus said to them, "Don't you understand this parable? How then will you understand any parable?" ' (Mark 4:13).

There is no conflict between the evangelists here. It is simply that Mark recalls the challenge in Jesus' tone at this time. Jesus' rebuke drives this truth home: if you do not grasp the basic point here, you will fail to understand any parable.

Mark's introduction of Jesus' words makes this clear. Apart even from the fact that these simple, 'visual' truths will be a closed book to the outsider, if the follower fails to grasp the method behind the story-telling, then the message will be lost on him too. Even the method remains a mystery. Access to the information on the computer is barred because the password is unknown. The glorious secret of the kingdom, with all its transforming power, is still a secret. Both, negatively, to resolve the riddle of the kingdom and, positively, to reveal its secret, the method of parables is crucial. This rebuke is not just for outsiders but for believers, Mark stresses. This is the principle behind parables, but what then is the password which gives access to the mystery?

The means — the Word of God

The password by which the kingdom is planted in the hearts of men is the Word of God. Jesus makes this clear in his explanation of the parable. This is where the rubber hits the road and the principle becomes practice. The deceptive simplicity of the story hides a depth of meaning: Jesus is the sower; the field is the world; the seed is the Word of God. It is summed up in Jesus' concise and graphic explanation: 'The farmer sows the word' (Mark 4:14).

The brevity of Mark's quotation of Jesus' words is typical. Substantially, that was what Jesus said. Luke gives the fuller form: 'The seed is the word of God' (Luke 8:11). Matthew says that it is 'the message about the kingdom' (Matt. 13:19). Jesus may well have included all three expressions but the point is the same and it is this point that grips Mark's mind as he recalls Jesus' teaching. That Mark uses the absolute term 'the word' is striking too, and he repeats it eight times in this section. On other occasions, Mark uses the terms 'gospel' and 'my words' (Mark 1:15; 8:35,38), but here it is the simple expression 'the word'. Later 'the Word' is used in the New Testament as a comprehensive description of all that is involved in the scriptural presentation of the truth about Jesus Christ. It is a term that stresses the divine power of the message, as a communication from God. It has its source in the mouth of God; it is what God says, and this is why it stands 'written' in Scripture. The image of seed simply enhances its authority. The power is inherent, intrinsic, explosive and dynamic. It produces germination, life, growth and fruitfulness. Power is writ large across Jesus' simple yet profound explanation of the parable.

Isaiah says,

As the rain and the snow
    come down from heaven,
and do not return to it
    without watering the earth
and making it bud and flourish,

so that it yields seed for the sower and bread for the
    eater,
so is my word that goes from my mouth:
    it will not return to me empty,
but will accomplish what I desire
    and achieve the purpose for which I sent it
                       (Isa. 55:10-11).

Later in the New Testament we find the apostle Peter picking up this analogy. Quoting Isaiah, Peter writes in his first
letter of the seed-like Word and its regenerative power:

For you have been born again, not of perishable seed,
but of imperishable, through the living and enduring word
of God. For,

    'All men are like grass,
        and all their glory is like the flowers of the field;
    the grass withers and the flowers fall,
        but the Word of the Lord stands for ever.'

And this is the word that was preached to you (1 Peter
1:23).

The seed, which is the Word, explodes to life in the soil of
man's soul. What an image of regeneration! The mysterious
fulfilment and the abiding fruitfulness of the seed-like Word
lie behind the dynamic power of Jesus' explanation: 'The farmer
sows the word' (Mark 4:14).

The authority of the Word is neither despotic nor dicta-
torial. Its sovereignty is tender. It does not barge into our lives
unbidden. Rather, like the seed, it requires suitable conditions
for germination and growth. This is the amazing thing about
Jesus' explanation. It is possible, given certain circumstances,

for this powerful Word of God to be ineffective! In only one case in the parable are germination and growth totally successful. But this takes nothing away from the sovereignty of the Word. The problem lies not with the seed but with the soil and the outcome depends upon the decree of God.

Calvin writes, 'This must be carefully observed, that we may not suppose the favours of God to cease to be what they are, though the good effect of them does not reach us. With respect to God, the Word is sown in the hearts, but it is far from being true that the hearts of all receive with meekness what is planted in them, as James (1:21) exhorts us to receive the Word. So then, the gospel is always a fruitful seed as to its power but not as to its produce.'

It is the relationship of the soil to the seed that determines effectiveness, or the lack of it. The plain truth is that the message of the kingdom is conveyed through the instrumentality of the Word. It may meet with indifferent success but this is the divinely specified way. Jesus gives his disciples the words his Father has given him. They accept the words, know with certainty that Jesus came from God and believe that God sent him (John 17:8). Paul says that 'Faith comes from hearing the message, and the message is heard through the word of Christ' (Rom. 10:17). James recalls that God 'chose to give us birth through the word of truth, that we might be a kind of first-fruits of all he created' (James 1:18). Peter claims that his hearers 'have been born again, not of perishable seed, but of imperishable, through the living and enduring word of God,' the word that was preached to them (1 Peter 1:23-25; cf. Isa. 40:6-8). The outward and ordinary means of communicating the gospel is through the Word. The Word is living and active and it has power: 'The farmer sows the word' (Mark 4:14).

Mark's presentation of Jesus' introductory rebuke and his terse description of the farmer sowing the Word stress the method of Jesus' parables both in principle and practice. How relevant the consideration of the Word is to our day too! Why do folk sit for a lifetime in church services, know the theory, 'understand' the truth and yet never come to faith in Christ? Why do others confronted by the same gospel seem to be listening but not really hearing? The answer on both counts is the absence of *divine* revelation to their hearts (Matt. 16:17). They have never seen Jesus as 'dynamic Prophet', the very Word of God. This is the truth implicit in the parable. The Word of God is not defective, but their hearing of it is not mixed with faith. Hearing it has become a human exercise like listening to a lecture.

For far too long evangelical Christianity has honed the expertise of her communicators and plied the methods of the mass-media in the service of the gospel, thinking that the traditional methods of preaching the Word and praying for its success are outmoded and failing. We need to recall Jesus' teaching here, not with gloom and depression but with excitement. Jesus is the dynamic Prophet — it is *he* who tills the ground, sows the seed, sends rain and sun and brings new life!

'The Spirit of God maketh the reading, but especially the preaching of the Word, an effectual means of convincing and converting sinners, and of building them up in holiness and comfort, through faith, unto salvation' (*Shorter Catechism,* 89).

The meaning — regeneration

In the message of the parables, Jesus explains the nature of the kingdom; by the method of the parables, he reveals the mystery of the kingdom; through the means implied in the interpretation, the Word of God, he shows the way of access to the kingdom; from the meaning of the parables, he discloses the miracle of the kingdom — regeneration. Mark presents Jesus' dynamic teaching of the parables so that these truths particularly emerge. The miracle of regeneration is clearly seen in the parable of the growing seed: 'He also said, "This is what the kingdom of God is like. A man scatters seed on the ground. Night and day, whether he sleeps or gets up, the seed sprouts and grows, though he does not know how. All by itself the soil produces corn — first the stalk, then the ear, then the full grain in the ear. As soon as the grain is ripe, he puts the sickle to it, because the harvest has come" ' (Mark 4:26-29).

Only Mark mentions this parable. Why does Mark record this story where he does, and what is he saying to us in his presentation?

The power of grace

The very setting of the parable in Mark helps us answer this question. The parable of the growing seed comes immediately after that of the sower. There are marked contrasts between the two. In the parable of the sower, human activity is to the fore — the reaction of the soil to the seed. In the parable of the growing seed, divine activity is secretly implicit — the seed grows regardless of man's sleeping or working. In the story of the sower, germination and growth, or the lack of it, are crucial to the tale. In the case of the growing seed, growth continues and harvest is introduced. In the account of the sower, Satan plays a destructive role. In that of the growing seed, God in the background mysteriously produces the growth quite independently of man. The parable of the growing seed stresses the secret power of the sovereignty of grace in regeneration.

Further, Mark uses the parable of the growing seed to introduce the parable of the mustard seed. The means whereby the 'smallest seed' becomes 'the largest of all garden plants' is a mysterious phenomenon of gradual growth. Mark is stressing the secret power of Jesus' divine grace not only in regeneration and growth, but in the harvest situation as well.

The potential of grace

If Mark discloses the power of God's grace in the *context* of the parable of the growing seed, he shows the potential of this grace in the *content* of the parable. There is the same air of mystery to this as there is in Jesus' words to Nicodemus about spiritual rebirth. Whether the man sleeps or gets up, the seed sprouts and grows. It does this all by itself, spontaneously. The man does not know how this comes about.

Mark is not stressing a lack of concern on the part of the farmer. That would be to turn the parable into an allegory and to push the imagery too far. Rather, Mark is underlining the divine potential in the seed and the regenerative power contained within it. This sprouting and growing are independent of human effort. They are divinely caused. The potential of the sovereignty of the Lord Jesus' divine grace in regeneration is supernatural. As it is in the natural realm, so it is in the spiritual. Salvation belongs to God at its beginning, middle and close; in the seed, the stalk, the ear and the full kernel. Jesus spoke with authority. In presenting these parables, he shows that he is the author of this miracle of divine grace.

It was late one evening and I did not feel much like visiting, but I did go. A mother had told me about her son Ken and his wife, who would both appreciate a visit from the minister. Eventually I called and the exciting saga began. Ken and his wife started attending church regularly. I thought I discerned interest and I called at the home again. Ken wanted to talk. What he had learned of Scripture at school was beginning to come back to him, but in a different way. He had, in the past, given up going to church, but now the Word was becoming vital to him, its message challenging. Would I, from Scripture, help him to see the key message of the Bible, in particular the nature of faith and how to gain it? Were there role models he could follow? Delighted, I set about the task. I specified some New Testament characters, left the passages with him to study and gave him appropriate questions to ponder. Ken did so and his interest grew. Issues were clarified, questions answered, terms explained, problems resolved.

Weeks passed, but this much was clear: germination was taking place. We did not rush matters, but eventually Ken came to faith. He read Mark's Gospel, then John's Gospel, started attending the church services and the mid-week meeting. Growth was taking place. At each stage, always it was the Word working, whether in sowing, germination or growth. Ken ultimately expressed interest in church membership. It had all been so worthwhile. It had all happened in terms of the parable of the sower. In so many other cases, the seed had been snatched away, or the growth was superficial or stunted. But not so in Ken's case. There it was gloriously successful. How we should pray for more of this: the life is in the stump; the remnant will be saved.

The message is about the kingdom, the method is a mystery disclosed, the means is the Word of God, and the success is sometimes apparently limited. But it is all exactly as Jesus taught. Mark underlines this in his Gospel.

> Almighty God, thy Word is cast
> Like seed into the ground
> Now let the dew of heaven descend,
> And righteous fruits abound.
>
> Let not the foe of Christ and man
> This holy seed remove,
> But give it root in every heart
> To bring forth fruits of love.

Let not the world's deceitful cares
The rising plant destroy,
But let it yield a hundredfold
The fruits of peace and joy.

Oft as the precious seed is sown,
Thy quickening grace bestow,
That all whose souls the truth receive
Its saving power may know.

                              (John Cawood, 1775-1852)

4.
Controversial Teacher

Each Gospel writer gives his particular emphasis to the on-going controversy with the religious leaders during Jesus' ministry. Mark adds his own distinctive note. After recounting some early skirmishes with the scribes (or teachers of the law) and Pharisees, involving disputes over the Sabbath and fasting, Mark gives a condensed account of a further controversy about washing (Mark 2:1 - 3:6; 7:1-23). It all savours of Mark's style: it is concise, clear, detailed but not flamboyant, direct but not crude, simple but not simplistic. Mark plainly has Gentiles in mind among his readers, for he explains Jewish terms which Matthew takes as read. Mark's comments, given in brackets (e.g. Mark 7:3-4,11), spell out the meaning and become as important as the narrative to which they are attached. Mark's 'asides' are of the utmost significance.

Controversy with the scribes and Pharisees plays a large part in all the Gospel accounts. Matthew's treatment of the topic has the usual distinctive Jewish flavour which marks his Gospel. His catalogue of 'woes' against the scribes and Pharisees recalls the curses uttered against God's people from Mount Ebal for breaking the law at the close of Deuteronomy (Matt. 23:1-39; cf. Deut. 27:9-26). Matthew's treatment of controversy is expansive and fulsome. Luke, with his more personal touch, locates Jesus' attack on the leaders in the home of a Pharisee, where he had been asked to dine (Luke 11:37-54).

Mark sets the scene of controversy. Like Matthew, he mentions the deputation of religious leaders who came from Jerusalem to interrogate Jesus (Mark 7:1-23; cf. Matt. 15:1-20). The context is formal, not personal like that in Luke. But Mark's account at this point is much more detailed, forceful and explanatory than Matthew's. He is not only explaining details of Jewish ritual to Gentile readers but making points of profound principle.

The context of the controversy is striking. Just as after his presentation of Jesus' use of parables Mark cites three miracles reflecting Jesus' power (Mark 4:1 - 6:6), so after Mark's account of controversy he relates three miraculous incidents (Mark 7:1 - 8:26). All this indicates that the gospel is not just for Jews but for Gentiles as well. In view of this, Mark's asides and explanations are crucial to interpreting what is going on. Jesus is exploding the restrictive nature of Jewish legalism and demonstrating the universal outreach of his message.

Their religion was outward in form

Mark shows how Jesus regards the legalism of the scribes and Pharisees as merely a matter of outward form. The first debate involves ceremonial cleansing, or Jewish rites of purification. The Old Testament spoke plainly of these matters. Ceremonial defilement barred not only from the service of the sanctuary but from fellowship with others. Contact with a dead body, leprosy, both natural and unnatural reproductive functions, and physical impairments all required purification (Num. 19:11-22; Lev. 12-15; 21:16-24). This principle affected not only persons but things. Utensils, beds, couches, tables and clothing were contaminated and had to be ritually cleansed (Lev. 11). It involved food also, for there were 'clean' and 'unclean' animals, through eating which defilement could come

(Lev. 11; Deut. 14). Persons, things, food — all came within the remit of this legislation, not only for priests and Levites, but for all the Israelites.

The problem, however, with the attitude of the scribes and Pharisees to the law was not one of neglect but of misreading its purpose. They made the law a matter of mere outward observance: 'The Pharisees and some of the teachers of the law who had come from Jerusalem gathered round Jesus and saw some of his disciples eating food with hands that were "unclean", that is, unwashed. (The Pharisees and all the Jews do not eat unless they give their hands a ceremonial washing, holding to the tradition of the elders. When they come from the market-place they do not eat unless they wash...)' (Mark 7:1-3).

These traditions not only bound the devotees with unnecessary restrictions; they spread the burden from people to things: 'And they observe many other traditions, such as the washing of cups, pitchers and kettles' (Mark 7:4).

An inward problem

Jesus exposes the external nature of their approach by prescribing internal change. He cuts through the detail of religious ceremonial to highlight the inner meaning behind the outer symbolism. He does this by showing that their traditions nullify the very law they purport to serve. Jesus inverts the entire order of the traditions: it is not what *goes into* a man but what *comes out of* a man that defiles him:

> Again, Jesus called the crowd to him and said, 'Listen to me, everyone, and understand this. Nothing outside a man can make him unclean by going into him. Rather, it is what comes out of a man that makes him unclean.'

After he had left the crowd and entered the house, his disciples asked him about this parable. 'Are you so dull?' he asked. 'Don't you see that nothing that enters a man from the outside can made him unclean? For it doesn't go into his heart but into his stomach, and then out of his body.' (In saying this, Jesus declared all foods clean) (Mark 7:14-19).

Jesus not only abolishes the old; he introduces the new. He gives the true meaning of the old. The list of sins Jesus mentions reflects the second table of the Ten Commandments. There is no distinction between the sinful intention and the sinful act: the one is as bad as the other. As Jesus taught elsewhere, the angry thought constitutes murder; the lustful look adultery (Matt. 5:21-30). Actual transgressions proceed from an evil nature. The problem is inward, a matter of the heart, not the stomach. So also is its cure. It requires change of heart, not observance of rite. This teaching is radical in the diagnosis it makes and in the cure it prescribes. 'He went on: "What comes out of a man is what makes him unclean. For from within, out of men's hearts, come evil thoughts, sexual immorality, theft, murder, adultery, greed, malice, deceit, lewdness, envy, slander, arrogance and folly. All these evils come from inside a man and make a man unclean" ' (Mark 7:20-23).

R. A. Finlayson sums up the matter thus: 'In the further teaching of Christ (see Mark 7:14-28) He transfers the set of defilement, and so of purity, entirely from the outer to the inner man. Purity in this sense may be said to be a state of heart reserved completely for God and freed from all worldly distractions.'

A universal principle

Mark not only underlines the fact that the Pharisees' insistence on ceremonial washing was typical of their whole legalistic approach to religion, but also shows that Jesus is here establishing a wider principle: 'In saying this, Jesus declared all foods clean' (Mark 7:19). He is underlining the wrong emphasis on the outward which characterizes Jewish legalism and the necessary inward reality that Jesus' kingdom requires. This shift of emphasis is, furthermore, not just a principle for Jewish readers but for Jew and Gentile. Jesus abolishes dietary ceremonial law for all time and for all people. He fulfils the law by abolishing it. Jesus' rule has a universal and abiding quality. His kingdom is spiritual and everlasting. In this Jesus fulfils all the types and shadows of the Old Testament and overrides the traditions set by the Jewish elders.

Even today people become absorbed in the externals of Christianity. A dependence on the rite of baptism; a superstitious concern about taking communion, as though the symbols conferred the grace; a false pride in saying prayers, reading the Scriptures and attending church — all of this majors on the externals and misses the inner reality. A distinction between the outward sign and the inner grace is lost. Religion becomes a matter of ritual observance. True holiness before God, through the forgiveness of sins and the imputation of Christ's righteousness, is absent. Personal fellowship with a holy God never comes into view. Belief becomes a form lacking substance. Ritualism replaces true religion.

An example from history

Martin Luther knew all about an outward religion. He recalls the barrenness of ritualism, on the one hand, and the exciting transformation of heart religion, on the other. The contrast in his words is a testimony to God's redeeming grace. The 'before and after' of his conversion experience is startling: 'All my brothers in the monastery who knew me will bear me out. If I had kept on any longer, I should have killed myself with vigils, prayers, reading and other work.' But then, 'I grasped that the justice of God is that righteousness by which through grace and sheer mercy God justifies through faith. Thereupon I felt myself to be reborn and to have gone through open doors into paradise. The whole of Scripture took on a new meaning, and whereas before "the righteousness of God" had filled me with hate, now it became to me inexpressibly sweet in greater love.'

For Martin Luther, the outward had become inward. The old had gone; the new had come. The malady was recognized and the prescribed cure worked. True religion replaced empty ritualism. Mark underlines this feature in his presentation.

Their religion was human in origin

Mark also points out how Jesus exposes the teaching of the religious leaders as human in origin. A commission representing the scribes and Pharisees arrives, sent to investigate the religion of Jesus and his followers. There are obvious differences of opinion needing to be resolved between the Jewish leadership and Jesus: 'So the Pharisees and teachers of the law asked Jesus, "Why don't your disciples live according to the tradition of the elders instead of eating their food with unclean hands?" ' (Mark 7:5).

The 'tradition of the elders'

But what was the 'tradition of the elders'? Was it simply hearsay customs handed down from one generation to another, known only to an inner circle, or was there anything behind these traditions? Indeed there was. The written Law of Moses was part of the Scriptures. The unwritten law, which Moses was *supposed* to have received on Sinai, was reputed to have been given orally by God to the elders. From this was formed the Talmud or 'doctrine'. The Talmud had two main parts.

First, there is the Mishnah, or 'repetitions' of the law. Then, there is the Gemara, or 'supplement' to it. There were constant additions to these. Such was the veneration for these traditions, it was said, 'The Law is like salt, the Mishnah like pepper, the Gemara like balmy spice.'

Jesus cuts through all of this. This time he confronts them over the source of their doctrine. Their traditions are human. Those stone tablets were the work of God; the writing was his writing, engraved on the tablets (Exod. 32:16). Man was not to live by bread alone but by every word which comes from the mouth of God (Deut. 8:3). Their teaching, while it claimed to come from the written law, was in many ways at variance with that law. This problem was even more serious than that of ritualism. The latter had reduced the law by externalizing it, but this removed the law by ignoring it. The commands of God were lost amid the details of human rules.

Jesus shows from Isaiah that their teachings were merely *human* rules (Isa. 29:13). The human origin of their teaching and their rigid adherence to it meant that they were setting aside God's Word and holding on to the traditions of men. They honoured God with their lips, but rejected him with their lives:

He replied, 'Isaiah was right when he prophesied about you hypocrites; as it is written:

' "These people honour me with their lips,
     but their hearts are far from me.
They worship me in vain;
     their teachings are but rules taught by men."

'You have let go of the commands of God and are holding on to the traditions of men' (Mark 7:6–8; cf. Isa. 29:13).

Acting a part

Jesus describes their attitude as hypocrisy. The Greek word *'hupocrites'* first meant someone who repeated words off by rote. Then it came to mean a 'play-actor'. The scribes and Pharisees, because they followed human teaching rather than the Word of God, were acting a part in a religious drama. There was an unreality about them. They were not what they claimed to be. God's Word alone produces a genuine life of faith. Man's philosophy produces counterfeit faith. It creates hypocrites.

It is often difficult for those who watch television 'soaps' to accept that the stars of these programmes are actors. The performers enter so imaginatively into their parts that we really think of them as husband and wife, or brother and sister, or teachers, or mechanics. The actors, too, feel themselves victims of their parts and frequently leave a particular programme on the grounds of being 'typecast'.

The human teaching of the scribes and Pharisees did just that. It produced actors whose performance was so persuasive that it was difficult, if not impossible, for people to distinguish them from true believers. They had typecast themselves. They had all the attributes and appearance of pious Jews, but they were in fact sham. There was a lack of reality about them. What made the difference was their doctrine. Had they been truly following God's Word, the result would have been otherwise. Then true piety and genuine godliness would have been evident. As it was, hypocrisy was present, because, for them, human rules had supplanted God's Word. Jesus goes to the very root of this problem. As a skilful surgeon, he diagnoses accurately and excises deftly the cancer of false teaching. As a masterful debater, he exposes the flawed nature of his opponents' reasoning by pointing to the inadequate source of their knowledge.

Setting aside God's commands

The leaders 'let go of the commands of God and are holding on to the traditions of men' (Mark 7:8). They do this intentionally: 'You have a fine way of setting aside the commands of God in order to observe your own traditions!' (Mark 7:9). 'Thus you nullify the word of God by your tradition that you have handed down' (Mark 7:13). In Mark we see the Lord Jesus as a 'controversial teacher' affirming the Word of God, without watering down its meaning for fear of consequences. Never must the Word of God be put on the same level as the traditions and utterances of men. To do so is utter blasphemy.

John Bunyan, in *Pilgrim's Progress*, links hypocrisy with formalism and relates both to false teaching. The issue in his story is that of entering into the kingdom. Formalist and Hypocrisy, contrary to following the way prescribed in Scripture, came in over the wall and not by the gate. Christian reasons with them, but they claim custom for their justification and regard it as irrelevant how they got into the kingdom:

CHRISTIAN. But will it not be counted a trespass against the Lord of the City whither we are bound, thus to violate his revealed will?

FORMALIST AND HYPOCRISY. They told him, that as for that, he needed not trouble his head thereabout; for what they did they had custom for; and could produce, if need were, testimony that would witness it for more than a thousand years.

CHRISTIAN. But, said Christian, will your practice stand a trial of law?

FORMALIST AND HYPOCRISY. They told him, that custom, it being of so long a standing as above a thousand years, would, doubtless, now be admitted as a thing legal by an impartial judge; and besides, said they, if

we get into the way, what's matter which way we get
in? If we are in, we are in; thou art but in the way,
who, as we perceive, came in at the gate; and we are
also in the way, that came tumbling over the wall;
wherein now is thy condition better than ours?

CHRISTIAN. I walk by the *rule* of my Master; you walk by
the rude working of your fancies. You are counted
thieves already, by the Lord of the way; therefore, I
doubt you will not be found true men at the end of
the way. You come in by yourselves without his direction; and shall go out by yourselves, without his mercy.

Formalist and Hypocrisy, like the scribes and Pharisees, walked
by 'the rude working of [their] fancies', not by the rule of the
Master. They let go of the commands of God and held on to
the traditions of men. Their religion was human in origin. It
produced hypocrites, not believers; actors, not real children
of God.

Their religion was wrong in interpretation

Mark indicates how Jesus exposed the teaching of the scribes
and Pharisees as wrong in its interpretation of Scripture. In
the ensuing debate Jesus shows that the traditional teachers
were more than just confused and mistaken; rather, they intentionally misled the people. Jesus takes as an illustration the
specific case of 'Corban'. But what was 'Corban', and how
did it conflict with the written law of God? The idea had been
developed in Jewish tradition.

The example of Corban

'Corban' was a Hebrew word meaning 'offering' or 'oblation'
to God. Mark, again in parenthesis, explains Corban as 'a gift

devoted to God' (Mark 7:11), using the Greek Word *'doron'*, a 'gift', to translate the Hebrew *'corban'*. To regard something which had been set aside as 'Corban' for normal or ordinary use would violate its sanctity, since it was wholly dedicated to God and to his service.

A regular formula in the Talmudic tracts *Nedarim* and *Nazir* is: 'Be it Corban from which you might have benefited by me.' This means that a gift, which might under normal circumstances benefit another, is 'Corban' or devoted to God. It is not free for 'charitable' use but restricted for God's use alone. A modern illustration might be, for example, a Christian who is unwilling to use his 'tithing' money, which he had dedicated to God, for some other purpose such as paying for the shopping of his widowed mother. It is 'Corban', set aside for God's use alone.

'Corban' had become an excuse among the Jews for the neglect of God-given obligations. As Jesus here quotes, children were using the process to evade rightful responsibility for parents. Their tradition was nullifying God's law, by setting it aside. In this case, the error was even more serious than in the previous instances. It tampered with the intention of the written law by reinterpreting its meaning. The underlying principle of divine law was vitiated by human tradition: 'And he said to them: "You have a fine way of setting aside the commands of God in order to observe your own traditions! For Moses said, 'Honour your father and your mother,' and 'Anyone who curses his father or mother must be put to death.' But you say that if a man says to his father or mother: 'Whatever help you might otherwise have received from me is Corban' (that is, a gift devoted to God), then you no longer let him do anything for his father or mother. Thus you nullify the Word of God by your tradition that you have handed down…" ' (Mark 7:9-13).

Further, Mark adds that such behaviour is characteristic of the scribes and Pharisees. They do this kind of thing all the time; misconstruing the law for their own advantage is second nature to them: 'And you do many things like that' (Mark 7:13).

Mark shows the detrimental effect of misconstruing the law in this way. His presentation of Jesus' teaching makes clear how radically the religious leaders tampered with God's law in order that they might bring about the very opposite result of what was originally intended. It is not only an arid, but a dangerous legalism. The hypocrite is a mere professor, not a possessor of faith.

The experience of John Wesley

For years, John Wesley had had an outward profession of faith, in which some of his beliefs in particular led to grave misconceptions as to the meaning of Scripture as a whole: 'I believe, till I was about ten years old I had not sinned away that "washing of the Holy Ghost" which was given me in baptism, having been strictly educated and carefully taught that I could only be saved "by universal obedience, by keeping all the commandments of God"; in the meaning of which I was diligently instructed. And these instructions, so far as they respected outward duties and sins, I gladly received and often thought of. But all that was said to me of inward obedience or holiness I neither understood nor remembered. So that I was indeed as ignorant of the true meaning of the Law as I was of the Gospel of Christ.'

This total misconception about biblical salvation was changed as the true nature of God's grace dawned on Wesley: 'In the evening I went very unwillingly to a society in Aldersgate Street, where one was reading Luther's preface to the Epistle to the Romans. About a quarter before nine, while he was describing the change which God works in the heart through faith in Christ, I felt my heart strangely warmed. I felt I did trust in Christ, Christ alone for salvation; and an assurance was given me that he had taken away *my* sins, even *mine*, and saved *me* from the law of sin and death.'

Wesley's misunderstanding of salvation was based on human traditions. He believed in baptismal regeneration and in justification by works. These traditions nullified the Word of God. In experiencing God's grace, his misconceptions were removed and the teaching of the Word of God became real to him personally. This resulted in a complete change from his view of salvation by works to one of salvation by grace. The former rested on human rules, the latter on the Word of God. From being a mere professor of religion, Wesley became a true possessor of the grace of God in Jesus Christ. This is what the Lord Jesus is saying in Mark. The traditions of the elders were used to nullify the Word of God for the sake of human convenience and selfishness. How we need once again to regain an understanding of this danger! The gospel of Christ is one which brings glory to God and not to man.

Their religion was restrictive in intent

Mark shows how the teaching of the religious leaders was restrictive in its intent. The restrictive nature of the teaching of the scribes and Pharisees is contrasted with the openness of the teaching of Jesus.

The gospel is for Gentiles too

Mark traces Jesus moving from conflict with the restrictiveness of Jewish legalism to a display of the power of the kingdom of God among the Gentiles in three incidents. He withdraws towards Tyre and Sidon, where he works a miracle for the daughter of a Greek Syro-Phoenician woman (Mark

7:24-30). He then returns via Gentile Decapolis, where he heals
a deaf-and-dumb man (Mark 7:31-37). He then comes to
Bethsaida Julias, the capital of the district of Gaulantinis, within
the territory of Herod Philip. This again is an area with a Gentile as well as a Jewish population. Here he restores sight to a
blind man (Mark 8:22-26).

Mark places between these two miracles the healing and
feeding of a large crowd, the Pharisees' demand for a sign
from heaven and Jesus' warning against the leaven of the Pharisees (Mark 8:1-21). It is as though Jesus is saying, 'Here is the
sign from heaven. Here is proof of my Messianic nature. Here
is the real answer to the restrictiveness of your religious leaders. Crowds are miraculously healed and fed, the blind see,
the deaf hear, the dumb speak. Not only among Jews but among
Gentiles too, the glory of the Lord has been revealed just as
Isaiah foretold.'

The kingdom has come

From the very sequence of these incidents Mark is sounding
the death-knell of narrow Jewish legalism and heralding the
dawn of good news for Gentiles as well as Jews. The kingdom
has come for all nations in Jesus Christ. Here then is the fulfilment of Isaiah 35:5- 6:

>   Then will the eyes of the blind be opened
>   and the ears of the deaf unstopped.
>   Then will the lame man leap like a deer
>   and the mute tongue shout for joy.
>   Water will gush forth in the wilderness
>   and streams in the desert.

In Mark's picture of Christ as the controversial Teacher,
Jesus condemns the religion of the scribes and Pharisees as

outward in form, human in origin and wrong in interpretation. Traditionalism produces ritualists, hypocrites and mere professors of religion. Jesus cuts through the sham of traditionalism, and shows that God's law is inward and spiritual in content and divine in power. Jesus is the true Law-giver. What the law could not do because of the weakness of the sinful nature, Christ accomplishes. Jesus both fulfils and abolishes God's law in his own perfect person and redeeming work. Jesus shows that his kingdom is not restricted within the narrow confines of Judaism, but the gospel is for all men. The kingdom has come in Jesus of Nazareth. The mystery of the kingdom is now resolved, the secret revealed. The old world of Jewish ceremonial has gone for ever, fulfilled and abolished in Christ, the controversial teacher. Mark says all of this in his own unique portrayal of Jesus. Has his message reached our hearts? Are we only professors or actual possessors of the true religion of Jesus?

5.
Suffering Servant

Peter's confession at Caesarea Philippi is a watershed in the Gospels. Matthew, Mark and Luke all make that clear. It marks a new phase in the ministry of Jesus. Before that point Jesus preaches, heals and debates with the religious leaders throughout Judea. From then on the momentum changes. Jerusalem comes into view. The cross throws its shadow over every page. Affairs speed quickly to their dramatic and horrific end.

Caesarea Philippi also marks a change of emphasis in Jesus' teaching. Up to then, instruction had been to the people in general, calling them to enter the kingdom, confirming this through miracles, expounding the message of the kingdom. From now on Jesus concentrates on teaching his disciples. He would have them understand the purpose of his mission, who he is, why he came, what he will do. ' "But what about you?" he asked. "Who do you say I am?" ' (Mark 8:29). The keynote is intense, intimate and personal. From Caesarea Philippi onwards, Jesus portrays Daniel's 'Son of Man' figure in terms of Isaiah's 'suffering Servant' and applies these prophecies to himself as Messiah.

William Lane says, 'In no other Gospel do the three cardinal announcements of forthcoming humiliation have as structured a function as they do in Mark. They furnish the framework, the tone and the subject of Chapters 8:31 - 10:52. The primary purpose of this section is to explain what it means

for Jesus to be the Messiah and what it requires to be identified with him. In the movement of the Gospel it serves to bring
Jesus near Jerusalem where his suffering will be accomplished.'

Three lessons concerning Jesus' forthcoming suffering,
death and resurrection are recounted in quick succession, in
chapters 8, 9 and 10. The necessary death, glorious resurrection and ransoming sacrifice of the Messiah are set forth. Each
lesson has its own significant setting: the first at Caesarea
Philippi, the second on the Mount of Transfiguration and the
third on the road to Jerusalem (Mark 8:27 - 9:1; 9:2-32;
10:32-52).

The secret as to who Jesus is and what he will do, relatively
hidden in the first part of Mark's Gospel, is now disclosed
through these private lessons. The mission of Jesus as Messiah, what is required of those who follow him and the continuing lack of understanding on the part of the disciples are
all emphasized. The focus is on Jesus as the suffering Servant.
Again, we gaze with awe at this Christ, and are encouraged to
personal faith in him.

Mark brings us to the challenge of the gospel. As long as
we stand on the sidelines of the story, interested, even admir-
ing, but uninvolved, we fail to experience its vital impact. Jesus
must step out of the Bible to us as a real person and confront
our lives with who he is, why he came and what he will do in
us. And we must respond to him, for we cannot remain indifferent. All through the Gospel, Mark is leading up to this. The
question that comes hauntingly from start to finish is: 'But
what about you? ... Who do you say I am?' (Mark 8:29). It is
a question that each reader must answer individually.

The necessity of his death

The first of those three lessons takes place just after Peter's
confession at Caesarea Philippi. This marks the beginning of

Jesus' instruction of his disciples. The lesson is the necessity of the Messiah's death. Jesus teaches through a series of contrasts.

The location

There was contrast in the location. Caesarea Philippi was a strange yet striking place for such a lesson. The source of the Jordan was said to be in that region. It was outside Galilee, under the jurisdiction of Philip, not Herod. It had a remarkable history. Its old name was Balinas, for it was a centre of Baal worship, and it was a centre for the worship of the Greek god Pan. Also, on the hillside where Caesarea was situated, Philip the tetrarch had built a temple of white marble in honour of Caesar. So the cult of emperor worship was practised there. Caesarea was a 'multi-faith centre'. What an odd place for a Galilean fisherman to confess that a wandering Jewish teacher was Messiah!

Contrasting views of Christ

First, there was the difference between Peter's opinion of Jesus and that of people in general:

> Jesus and his disciples went on to the villages around Caesarea Philippi. On the way he asked them, 'Who do people say I am?'
>
> They replied, 'Some say John the Baptist; others say Elijah, and still others, one of the prophets.'
>
> 'But what about you?' he asked. 'Who do you say I am?'
>
> Peter answered, 'You are the Christ.'
>
> Jesus warned them not to tell anyone about him (Mark 8:27-30).

Secondly, there was the contrast between Peter's perception of the Messiah's mission and Jesus' own view:

> He then began to teach them that the Son of Man must suffer many things and be rejected by the elders, chief priests and teachers of the law, and that he must be killed and after three days rise again. He spoke plainly about this, and Peter took him aside and began to rebuke him.
>
> But when Jesus turned and looked at his disciples, he rebuked Peter. 'Get behind me, Satan!' he said. 'You do not have in mind the things of God, but the things of men' (Mark 8:31-33).

Thirdly, there was the contrast between the popular ideas of Messiah and Jesus' self-revelation:

> Then he called the crowd to him along with his disciples and said: 'If anyone would come after me, he must deny himself and take up his cross and follow me. For whoever wants to save his life will lose it, but whoever loses his life for me and for the gospel will save it. What good is it for a man to gain the whole world, yet forfeit his soul? Or what can a man give in exchange for his soul? If anyone is ashamed of me and my words in this adulterous and sinful generation, the Son of Man will be ashamed of him when he comes in his Father's glory with the holy angels' (Mark 8:34-38).

Mark here mentions a feature which Matthew omits, the consequences of being ashamed of Jesus and his Word (Mark 8:38). Mark is underlining the cost of discipleship.

A secret revealed

As Jesus goes on to apply the challenge of his death for those who would follow him, the three evangelists introduce the teaching like this: 'Then Jesus said to his disciples...' (Matt. 16:24); 'Then he said to them all...' (Luke 9:23); 'Then he called the crowd to him along with his disciples and said...' (Mark 8:34). Matthew refers the teaching to the disciples. Luke is more indefinite. But Mark is quite specific as to who the audience is. Jesus, at that point, moves from private to public, calls the crowd to hear him and shares teaching with them. His words teach the reality of the kingdom of God coming 'with power'.

It is as though Mark is saying, 'Up to now the story has been shrouded with secrecy by the Lord Jesus himself. He lived, taught and acted in this way. He did so to show that he was the real Messiah, not some political activist, whose only motive was to free the Jews from the Romans and establish a national kingdom. Rather, Jesus is a spiritual Messiah, who releases men from Satan's grip of sin and establishes the kingdom of God in their lives.'

That is the reason for the secrecy of his teaching through parables and the requests for secrecy after his miraculous acts. But now things are quite different and Peter's confession marks the point of change. Now Jesus is openly frank with his disciples. Now he systematically teaches them the necessity of his death, to prove to them that he is the real Messiah. The Son of Man is the suffering Servant of Isaiah.

This is not simply for his disciples. The message of the necessity of Christ's death is for all men. Immediately after he informs the disciples of his death, he speaks to all men of the necessity of following him and what is involved in it. Those demands include a recognition of the need for 'the cross', or the Messiah's death. In some strange way this will become part of their lives as they live or die as his followers. He also links these requirements to himself and his words, words of which his followers need never be ashamed. Those requirements mean that it is he, the Christ, and not the world, who is to rule their lives. Jesus calls all men, not just his disciples, to see the necessity of his death and the cost of discipleship. The Messiah *must* die.

A hard truth to accept

Humanly speaking, this will not do. Generations of pious Jews could accept as Messiah an anointed Son of David who would destroy God's enemies and bring in a golden age for Jerusalem and God's people. They could envisage a Messiah fulfilling Daniel's vision of a glorious Son of Man who would represent the people before God. But a Messiah who would be put to death was unacceptable to them. Jesus recalls Isaiah's Servant as he explains his own mission as Son of Man. Isaiah's Servant *must* die for his people:

> But he was pierced for our transgressions,
>   he was crushed for our iniquities;
> the punishment that brought us peace was upon him,
>   and by his wounds we are healed.
> By oppression and judgement he was taken away.
>   And who can speak of his descendants?
> For he was cut off from the land of the living;
>   for the transgression of my people he was stricken.
> He was assigned a grave with the wicked,
>   and with the rich in his death,
> though he had done no violence,
>   nor was any deceit in his mouth
>
> (Isa. 53:5,8-9).

My friend could neither understand nor accept why Jesus had to die. She was of mature years and by no means unintelligent. She was interested enough to come to our services and wanted to enquire further into the whole matter. But this was where her mental block to the gospel occurred. There was a contrast between her traditional view of a Christianity in which Jesus taught and healed and a gospel where Jesus had to die. It was a gulf she simply could not span.

I had met the problem before, but only theoretically. Now I faced it in real life and it taught me some important lessons. Only when she came to recognize her own sinfulness and her need of the atoning death of Jesus would this lady accept the necessity of the cross. Until then, the whole gospel was both illogical and, understandably, irrelevant. The necessity of Messiah's death lies at the very heart of the gospel. Eventually she saw this and became a Christian.

Jesus began by teaching his disciples these things. But they, let alone the crowd of outsiders, failed to grasp its truth. Even Peter failed, in spite of his remarkable confession at Caesarea. Have you failed to grasp the necessity of Jesus' death for your own salvation?

The glory of his resurrection

The second lesson followed about a week later on the occasion of Christ's transfiguration. This second lesson was equally perplexing for the disciples. It argued the rising of the Son of Man from death. The Messiah who must die rises gloriously. The message moves from despair to hope, from gloom to glory.

The transfiguration described

There was an eerie mystery about the mountain where Jesus

was transfigured. Both Matthew and Mark call it a 'high' mountain. We tend to think of Jesus and his three friends walking up a little hillock. This was not the case; it was a 'mountain-top experience' in every sense of the word. The appearance of Moses, giver of the law, recalls the fearfulness of Mount Sinai. The sight of Elijah, champion among the prophets, echoes the victory on Mount Carmel. The cloud, the symbol of God's presence to the Jew, envelops the group in mist. A voice from heaven resounds in those surroundings, affirming Jesus to be not only David's kingly Son and Isaiah's beloved Servant, but also the Prophet promised to Moses: 'This is my Son, whom I love. Listen to him!' (Mark 9:7; cf. Ps. 2:7; Isa. 42:1; Deut. 18:15). Peter, overcome with fear, blurts out his request to erect three shelters.

And he said to them, 'I tell you the truth, some who are standing here will not taste death before they see the kingdom of God come with power.'

After six days Jesus took Peter, James and John with him and led them up a high mountain, where they were all alone. There he was transfigured before them. His clothes became dazzling white, whiter than anyone in the world could bleach them. And there appeared before him Elijah and Moses, who were talking with Jesus.

Peter said to Jesus, 'Rabbi, it is good for us to be here. Let us put up three shelters — one for you, one for Moses and one for Elijah.' (He did not know what to say, they were so frightened).

Then a cloud appeared and enveloped them, and a voice came from the cloud: 'This is my Son, whom I love. Listen to him!'

Suddenly, when they looked round, they no longer saw anyone with them except Jesus (Mark 9:1-8).

What did 'rising from the dead' mean?

Coming down, they discussed the questions posed on the
mountain. Jesus himself introduced the debate. He told them
to say to no one what they had seen until the Son of Man had
risen from the dead. He had commanded the same silence at
Caesarea. But the need for silence was not now the greatest
problem for them. It was the Son of Man 'rising from the
dead' that they did not understand. A murdered Messiah was
unacceptable. A Messiah risen from the dead was simply
incredible.

They began to discuss what 'rising from the dead' meant.
People claimed that Jesus was Elijah. But they had just seen
Elijah. The prophet Malachi spoke of a risen Elijah; he mentioned Moses too: 'Remember the law of my servant Moses,
the decrees and laws I gave him at Horeb for all Israel. See, I
will send you the prophet Elijah before that great and dreadful
day of the LORD comes. He will turn the hearts of the fathers
to their children, and the hearts of the children to their fathers;
or else I will come and strike the land with a curse' (Mal.
4:4-5).

Jesus quietly adds to the earlier truth he taught. The forerunner has already come. Now the Messiah, the Son of Man,
must suffer, die and rise again. But who is this Son of Man?
Where does Scripture speak of the Messiah suffering, dying
and rising? Eventually, they would find the answer, not in Elijah,
but in Isaiah's prophecy of the Servant who suffers and dies
and who will rise again:

> Yet it was the LORD's will to crush him and cause him to
>   suffer,
>   and though the LORD makes his life a guilt offering,
> he will see his offspring and prolong his days,
>   and the will of the LORD will prosper in his hand.

> After the suffering of his soul,
>> he will see the light [of life] and be satisfied
>>>>> (Isa. 53:10-11).

That lay too far in the future for them now. Later, they would see it, but not now: ' "The Son of Man is going to be betrayed into the hands of men. They will kill him, and after three days he will rise." But they did not understand what he meant and were afraid to ask him about it' (Mark 9:31-32).

Who would rise?

> As they were coming down the mountain, Jesus gave them orders not to tell anyone what they had seen until the Son of Man had risen from the dead. They kept the matter to themselves, discussing what 'rising from the dead' meant.
> And they asked him, 'Why do the teachers of the law say that Elijah must come first?'
> Jesus replied, 'To be sure, Elijah does come first, and restores all things. Why then is it written that the Son of Man must suffer much and be rejected? But I tell you, Elijah has come, and they have done to him everything they wished, just as it is written about him' (Mark 9:9-13).

Mark stresses two things in particular: the resurrection of the Son of Man and the lack of understanding of this on the part of the disciples. Mark stresses these more than Matthew and Luke. He alone defines precisely the terms of that discussion as they came down the mountain. Luke omits any reference to it. Mark couches it in these terms: 'They kept the matter to themselves, discussing what rising from the dead meant' (Mark 9:10).

'Rising from the dead' was uppermost in their minds, even though Elijah came into that discussion. What a subject that must have been! How confused their minds were about that! It was not the *idea* of resurrection that was the problem. They could glean enough from their Jewish Old Testament upbringing to take that on board. It was rather *who* should rise from the dead? Who was the Son of Man who would rise from the dead?

The prophet Malachi spoke of Elijah coming before that great day of the Lord and turning the hearts of God's people. Elijah obviously would have to rise and come back to do that. The rabbis said that Elijah would come three days before the Messiah. On the first day he would cry, 'Peace comes to the world'; on the second, 'Good comes to the world'; on the third, 'Salvation comes to the world'. But they had just seen Elijah along with Moses, so who was the Son of Man who would rise from the dead?

As Jesus went on to tell them that Elijah had already come and that he had been treated as Scripture predicted, they were left with few alternatives. Clearly Jesus was not Elijah risen from death, though some claimed he was. If Elijah had come, and he, they might deduce, was John the Baptist, then the Son of Man must be Jesus himself. This would mean that it would indeed be he, as he had been telling them, who would suffer, die and after three days rise again. The necessary death would lead to a glorious resurrection. But still, they did not like the idea. Could it really be so?

The need for more faith

Mark describes their encounter with the youth with the evil spirit whom they met after coming down the mountain. Mark is more detailed in his report of this than Matthew and Luke.

Mark mentions not only a great crowd of people being present, as Matthew and Luke do, but also scribes present and debating the matter. Mark twice records horrific details of the youth's affliction, compared to a single mention by Matthew and Luke. Mark records that the youth's father did believe, but cried for his remaining unbelief to be removed. Mark attributes the powerlessness of the disciples to heal the boy not only to 'little faith', as did Matthew, but to inactive faith: 'This kind can come out only by prayer' (Mark 9:29). Above all, while Matthew and Luke describe Jesus' treatment of the boy as 'healing', Mark depicts the youth, in the eyes of the crowd, as 'dead' and Jesus' action in taking him by the hand and lifting him up, as in a real sense, 'raising' him!

These details are significant. Of course, each Gospel writer is contrasting the power of Christ on the mountain with the powerlessness of the disciples on the plain. But Mark is emphasizing the power of resurrection and the disciples' lack of understanding of his own particular purpose. Jesus is the Son of Man and he will rise the third day. They do 'believe' in Jesus, just as the boy's father 'believed' in his son's healing, but their remaining unbelief has to be dislodged so that they can both understand and accept the necessity of the death and resurrection of Jesus, as God's way of inaugurating his kingdom. Their faith needed help to see as its true object and foundation the death and resurrection of Jesus. Often we need that help too.

Mark concludes this second lesson with Jesus' prophecy of the Son of Man's betrayal, death and resurrection after three days and then the disciples' lack of understanding and fear to enquire further (Mark 9:31-32). Mark, more than all the evangelists, is emphasizing that the Jesus who must die rises gloriously. Each must respond to that with personal faith.

A *personal testimony*

I remember from boyhood the impact Christ's resurrection made on me. There were the Easter Day services when we sang joyfully, 'Jesus Christ is risen today, Hallelujah!', the sermons that recalled the empty tomb, empty grave-clothes, resurrection appearances, burning hearts on the road to Emmaus and the transformed and rejuvenated disciples. Then came university, the talks in the Christian Union, sifting the evidence, objectively weighing the pros and cons: the veracity of the witnesses, the absence of the body, the tone and statements of Scripture, the swoon theory, the possibilities of hallucinations, or a metaphysical explanation. Then at theological college came the consideration of the context of the resurrection in Scripture, the doctrinal significance, the evidence re-examined and, of course, private reading.

I needed to be convinced of Christ's resurrection, not just because I had always been taught it, or because it felt good, or exciting, or half-reasonable to believe. But I needed to know that it was true, that it really did happen. Then I read Frank Morison's *Who moved the Stone?* The author, a law student at the turn of the century, when the historicity of Jesus was under attack in many circles, impressed me. Morison admired Jesus as a character, but had serious doubts as to the trustworthiness of the Gospel records, particularly those concerning the last week of Jesus' life and especially those about his resurrection. He set about writing a book to disprove the resurrection. That book was never written. Instead, examining the evidence, Frank Morison was convinced of the glorious truth of the resurrection of Jesus and was converted. He wrote *Who moved the Stone?*, a remarkable affirmation of the truth of Jesus' resurrection. Morison's primary witness was that of Scripture itself. That book helped confirm the resurrection to me in an exciting way.

A fundamental truth

What a tragedy that so many church leaders disbelieve the resurrection! The resurrection is so fundamental, so basic to the gospel that to dispense with it or explain it away pulls the foundation stone from the base of Christianity itself: 'And if Christ has not been raised, your faith is futile; you are still in your sins' (1 Cor. 15:17). There are no options on this issue for the Christian, let alone for the Christian leader. The resurrection is either glorious truth or foolish error. Jesus, in that second lesson to his disciples — dispirited as they were at the knowledge of Messiah's necessary death and now baffled at the prospect of his resurrection — made that abundantly clear: 'They will kill him, and after three days he will rise' (Mark 9:31). The disciples' lack of understanding then we can easily grasp. Their subsequent acclamation of his glorious resurrection transformed their lives. We must discuss and debate the issues from the truth of Scripture, as Jesus himself commands, but must ultimately be convinced individually, through the Holy Spirit, of what was written about him. We have no alternative but to accept and affirm the resurrection as absolute, literal truth. Christ was raised on the third day according to the Scriptures (1 Cor. 15:4).

The purpose of his death

The third lesson of Mark's Gospel is the climax of Jesus' teaching. Jesus now explains the reason for the death of the Son of Man. The Messiah who necessarily dies and gloriously rises gives his life as a ransoming sacrifice. That sacrifice is a debt discharged, a price paid, a ransom offered to liberate his people from the slavery of their sin. The Messiah's death is not only necessary but also voluntary. He offers up his life in willing sacrifice to God on behalf of his people. Jesus, who taught the necessity of his death in vivid contrasts and the glory of his resurrection through spirited discussion, now discloses the ransom offer of his sacrifice in a striking view of his person and a detailed preview of his work as Son of Man.

His determination to complete the work

Mark gives his three lessons, one after another, in chapters 8, 9 and 10. Furthermore, they are set in a tight geographical framework, describing Jesus' journey from Galilee to Jerusalem. Already in the village of Caesarea Philippi they are 'on the way' (Mark 8:27). They journey through Galilee, stopping off at Capernaum (Mark 9:30,33). Entering Judea at the lower Jordan they meet the rich ruler, when they are again 'on the way' (Mark 10:1,17). The third lesson is set in a context where they 'are going to Jerusalem' (Mark 10:32-34). Mark particularly notes these locations.

W. L. Lane comments: 'The meaning of the journey to Jerusalem is defined by the repeated announcements of Jesus' passion: he goes to Jerusalem to fulfil his Messianic destiny. He leads his disciples in the way of the cross by instructing them concerning the necessity of his sufferings and the requirement this imposes on them.'

We now find our Lord and his disciples on their way up to Jerusalem for the last time. Jerusalem itself comes into view. The scene is described by Mark in a particularly vivid way. Mark, alone of the evangelists, mentions that Jesus was 'out in front', leading the way, with the disciples following fearfully behind. The rabbi would normally lead his group like this, but there is something more at work here. Jesus presses forward, driven by an inner compulsion to get to Jerusalem, urgent to carry out the business in hand. The disciples, on the other hand, lag behind. Reluctance at the thought of their

Master's imminent death, and incredulity at his prediction of resurrection, dull their minds and make their feet leaden. Joyful anticipation of bringing the message of Jesus to the capital has now changed to fearful apprehension. Truth to tell, they do not want to go to Jerusalem — at least, not on Jesus' terms: 'They were on their way up to Jerusalem, with Jesus leading the way, and the disciples were astonished, while those who followed were afraid' (Mark 10:32).

Jesus presses on. His determination shows in his stance and in his face. Luke notes, earlier, how Jesus resolutely set out for Jerusalem: 'As the time approached for him to be taken up to heaven, Jesus resolutely set out for Jerusalem' (Luke 9:51). The same things were written of the determination of Isaiah's Servant:

> Because the Sovereign LORD helps me,
>   I will not be disgraced.
> Therefore have I set my face like flint,
>   and I know I will not be put to shame
>
> (Isa. 50:7).

Mark records this determination, as he introduces the final of Jesus' three lessons.

His sufferings foretold

In this lesson, Jesus recalls earlier instruction, but adds to it further details of what will happen to him. The Son of Man will be betrayed to the chief priests and scribes, sentenced to death and delivered to the Romans, who will mock, spit on him and scourge him (Mark 10:33-34). Treachery from the Jews, the involvement of the Gentiles, an orchestrated process of injustice, with Christ's arrest, flogging and execution, fill out the scant information of the two previous lessons.

Mark's unique portrayal of the redeeming work of Christ through his death is highlighted by his attention to the fulfilment of Jesus' words. Each item is fulfilled down to the very last detail in an intriguing and pointed way.

The predicted handing over of Jesus to the chief priests and scribes is fulfilled in Mark 14:53; the death sentence in Mark 14:64; the handing over to the Romans in Mark 15:1,10. Christ is mocked, spat upon, scourged in Mark 14:65; 15:15-20, executed in Mark 15:20-39,44 and raised from the dead in Mark 16:1-8. Indeed, Mark 15:15-20 gives the details of Mark 10:34 in reverse order and in fuller form.

The Son of Man as Isaiah's Servant

While the details of the third lesson recall the shame of the psalmist's righteous Sufferer (Ps. 22:6-8), they also clearly reflect the treatment meted out to Isaiah's righteous Servant. The mocking, spitting and scourging of Christ echo Isaiah's words:

> I offered my back to those who beat me,
>   my cheeks to those who pulled out my beard;
> I did not hide my face
>   from mocking and spitting
>
>   (Isa. 50:6).

The correspondence here between Jesus and Isaiah's Servant is unmistakable. It is even more so as Jesus responds to the request of James and John for preferential treatment for themselves. He states that the Son of Man 'did not come to be served, but to serve, and to give his life as a ransom for many' (Mark 10:45). The word 'ransom' recalls the Servant being 'offered for sin' (Isa. 53:10), and Jesus' use of the word 'many' reflects the 'many' whom the righteous Servant would justify

(Isa. 53:11,12). Indeed the whole sacrificial and substitutionary content of Isaiah 53 is echoed in this saying of Jesus.

Today, a ransom usually means the price paid to release someone who has been kidnapped. In Bible times the reference was wider. It spoke of the deliverance by purchase of a prisoner of war, slave or person condemned to death. It involved both sacrifice and substitution. Jesus' words here recall the fate of Isaiah's Servant in detail. This Servant sacrifices his life as a guilt-offering, pays the ultimate price by dying and substitutes for the many, who are transgressors:

> Yet it was the LORD's will to crush him and cause him to
> suffer,
> and though the LORD makes his life a guilt offering,
> he will see his offspring and prolong his days,
> and the will of the Lord will prosper in his hand...
> Therefore I will give him a portion among the great,
> and he will divide the spoils with the strong,
> because he poured out his life unto death
> and was numbered with the transgressors.
> For he bore the sin of many,
> and made intercession for the transgressors
>
> (Isa. 53:10,12).

The Son of Man is Isaiah's Servant. Jesus as Messiah must serve by giving his life as a ransom for many.

The cup and the baptism

Mark's record of this saying of Jesus is in the context of the request of James and John for pride of place in Jesus' kingdom (Matt. 20:20-28; Mark 10:35-45). The implication of all this is sadly plain. As Jesus enters the period of his ministry when the shadow of the cross looms darkest before him, his disciples strive among themselves for prime position. Even granted that James and John anticipate a triumphant Messianic banquet in Jerusalem with Jesus as host, this only underlines their continuing misconception as to what kind of Christ he was and what his kingdom was all about. They fail to grasp the essentials of his spiritual kingdom, and that their leader must suffer and die. They too would suffer for his sake. Christians often struggle for primacy within the church, when they should be taken up with seeking first the kingdom of God. How hurt Jesus must have been!

To drive home that suffering is involved in being a right-hand man in Jesus' kingdom, Matthew recalls Jesus' word describing his destiny as a 'cup'. Mark is doubly emphatic and also recalls Jesus' striking metaphor in which he describes his sufferings and death as a 'baptism'. Luke elsewhere mentions how Jesus viewed his suffering mission as 'a baptism to undergo' (Luke 12:50). But here, uniquely, Mark refers to these two vivid word-pictures of Jesus' ransoming sacrifice as both 'cup' and 'baptism':

> 'You don't know what you are asking,' Jesus said. 'Can you drink the cup I drink or be baptized with the baptism I am baptized with?'
>
> 'We can,' they answered.
>
> Jesus said to them, 'You will drink the cup I drink and be baptized with the baptism I am baptized with, but to sit at my right or left is not for me to grant. These places belong to those for whom they have been prepared' (Mark 10:38-40).

What do these pictures of the 'cup' and 'baptism' mean? Both imply experiencing the judgement of God. The 'cup' of God's wrath has that connotation in the Old Testament and is used by Jesus in Gethsemane referring to his own experience.

The 'baptism' has a parallel meaning. In the Old Testament it speaks of the watery ordeal of God's judgement. Jesus' own baptism carries that implication in the New Testament, as he identifies as a substitute for sinful man, bearing his punishment for sin. Both the psalmist and Isaiah use this imagery (Ps. 75:8; Isa. 51:17-23; Ps. 42:7; Isa. 43:2). The righteous Servant is one who identified with our sin to bring us peace (Isa. 53:5). The 'cup' and 'baptism' had added significance for Jesus which could never be experienced by James and John, but the sharing of suffering was common to all three. Mark, in recalling both images from the lips of Jesus, underscores the unique gravity of his suffering and death. Mark's particular record of the ransoming sacrifice of the Servant is that his sufferings were both a 'cup' he drank to the dregs and a 'baptism' with which he was baptized to the full.

A life given for others

P. C. Wren's novel *Beau Geste* always intrigued me. I read it years ago, saw it televised, then forgot the explanation of the plot and reread it recently to recover the excitement of this thriller. In the story, Beau or Michael Geste sacrifices his life in a far-flung outpost of the French Foreign Legion, claiming to have stolen an enormous sapphire called the 'blue water' which belonged to his erstwhile guardian Lady Brandon. In actual fact, Michael had not stolen this gem. Rather, hiding in a suit of armour years before, he had overheard Lady Brandon's plans to sell the 'blue water' to an oriental potentate, for she had fallen on difficult times, and decided to replace it with an imitation stone. The return of Lady Brandon's worthless husband, Lord Brandon, to find the imitation would have meant further misery for the good lady. So Michael, seeing it as the only way out of the impasse, stole the imitation and made off to the Foreign Legion claiming guilt. Michael's strange heroism in bearing the guilt of another's transgression meant literally that he gave his life as a ransom for others — Lady Brandon, his brothers Digby and John and his friends Isobel and Claudia. The story is a striking illustration of ransom on the human level. All the elements are there: an impossible situation, the only way of resolution in the ultimate sacrifice, the substitute bearing the guilt and distress of others and the explanation delayed to the end of the story.

On an infinitely greater and more righteous plane, Mark tells the story of Jesus' ransoming sacrifice for his people. There is the impossible plight of man in sin, the only resolution in the death of the Son of Man, the substitution for those who are transgressors and the intriguing delay of the full disclosure to the very end of the Gospel account. Only then does it become perfectly plain that Jesus is the Son of Man who offers his life as a ransoming sacrifice, necessarily dies and gloriously rises, and does so fulfilling the prophecy of Isaiah's suffering Servant. When that fact is grasped all the details fit into place:

> They were on their way up to Jerusalem, with Jesus leading the way, and the disciples were astonished, while those who followed were afraid. Again he took the Twelve aside and told them what was going to happen to him. 'We are going up to Jerusalem,' he said, 'and the Son of Man will be betrayed to the chief priests and teachers of the law. They will condemn him to death and will hand him over to the Gentiles, who will mock him and spit on him, flog him and kill him. Three days later he will rise.' ...
>
> When the ten heard about this, they became indignant with James and John. Jesus called them together and said, 'You know that those who are regarded as rulers of the Gentiles lord it over them, and their high officials exercise authority over them. Not so with you.

Instead, whoever wants to become great among you must be your servant, and whoever wants to be first must be slave of all. For even the Son of Man did not come to be served, but to serve, and to give his life as a ransom for many' (Mark 10:32-34,41-45).

Not only do we see in Mark's Gospel the necessary death, glorious resurrection and ransoming sacrifice of Jesus as Messiah, but we see the demands it makes on us. We see the need to accept the necessity of Christ's death personally for our sin if we are to go to heaven, to recognize the new life the risen Christ bestows and to come personally in repentance and faith to Christ. Without this, Mark's story is to us no more than a glorious but idle tale, an intriguing thriller with no saving content. The Holy Spirit, speaking through Mark, will not have it that way. What he writes is 'the gospel about Jesus Christ the Son of God'. This gospel requires us to respond to it. Mark tells his story in his own unique way for this specific purpose. Is Mark's Gospel lost on us?

6.
Majestic King

Jesus' ministry moves to its dramatic close. There had been the early days in Galilee, the brief interludes in coastal Tyre and mountainous Decapolis, the retreat to Caesarea and Mount Hermon. Now the party moved on again, southwards through troublesome Samaria, down the Jordan valley, via the dangerous Jericho road and finally to Jerusalem. How gloriously, yet fearfully, Jerusalem came into view, seen from the Mount of Olives or from the sleepy, warm, rural villages of Bethphage, the 'house of figs', and Bethany, the 'house of dates'. Lying ahead is Zion, with its temple and pilgrims, its Pharisees and Sadducees, its scribes and teachers. Jerusalem represents the end of the journey, the close of Christ's ministry.

> How glorious Sion's courts appear,
> The city of our God!
> His throne he hath established here,
> Here fixed his loved abode.
>
> Its walls, defended by his grace,
> No power shall e'er o'erthrow,
> Salvation is its bulwark sure
> Against the assailing foe.

Lift up the everlasting gates,
The door wide open fling;
Enter ye nations, who obey
The statutes of our King.

(Scottish Paraphrases, 20)

If ever Mark's tale was an eyewitness review of action-packed moments, it is so now. Events trip over one another in quick succession. There is scarcely time to tell it all. Days are packed full of significant happenings. Words give way to deeds. Teaching becomes intense. Things are moving towards crisis point. There is a sense of excitement mixed with foreboding. The end is near, whatever it may bring. Days of veiled secrecy as to who Jesus is and as to what he will do are now a thing of the past. It is all happening with such speed that it is hard to believe that those events filled only the days of one week. The scene is set for the final act of the unfolding drama.

Those events can be grouped in three: first, Jesus' triumphal entry to Jerusalem; second, his cursing of the fig tree together with his cleansing of the temple; and, third, Jesus' debates with the religious leaders. Three themes run through these three incidents: Jesus the royal King comes to the throne; Jesus the priestly King cleanses the temple; and Jesus the prophetic King silences the opposition.

The royal King comes to the throne

The triumphal entry is an acted parable of Jesus the royal King. It is the story of a rightful claimant coming to the throne and, in that very coming, portraying the nature of his kingdom. Jesus has planned it all and taken the initiative: the dispatch of the two disciples, the precise instructions as to where to find the colt, the details of the disciples' reply to be given to those who questioned them — all make this clear. Jesus, who had set his face to reach Jerusalem, was taking positive steps to implement the earlier lessons he had given them. The King had come to the heart of his kingdom.

Scripture prophecy fulfilled

The triumphal entry fulfilled Scripture too. Jesus' choice of animal was striking. The docile donkey was the beast of burden, the prancing stallion the mount of kings. But Jesus chose the donkey. This was exactly according to Zechariah's prediction:

>   Rejoice greatly, O Daughter of Zion!
>   Shout, Daughter of Jerusalem!
>   See, your king comes to you,
>   righteous and having salvation,
>   gentle and riding on a donkey,
>   on a colt the foal of a donkey
>
> (Zech. 9:9).

Through this Jesus is showing us the real Messiah, adding this visual aid to his earlier verbal witness that the Son of Man would suffer and die. The Messiah would come meekly to establish his kingdom. That was exactly how Zechariah had predicted it.

The reaction to the triumphal entry

The reaction of Jerusalem to Jesus' entry was remarkable. Cloaks were spread to saddle the donkey, clothing and branches to 'lay out the red carpet' along the King's path. Prayers and acclamations from Psalm 118 rang through the air: 'Hosanna!

Blessed is he who comes in the name of the Lord' (Mark 11:9; cf. Ps. 118:25-26). This was one of the Jews' *'Hallel'* or praise psalms. It was used frequently at the Feasts of Passover and Tabernacles — the Jews often thought of the Messiah as the 'Coming One'. The disciples now celebrated the miracles of Jesus as Messiah (Luke 19:37) and the children began to repeat what they had sung (Matt. 21:15). The religious rulers were livid. The world was going after him (John 12:19). The impact was incredible and the implication clear — Messiah had arrived.

So important is Jesus' entry to Jerusalem that all four Gospel writers mention it. Each tells it in his own way. Matthew recalls the fulfilment of Old Testament prophecy, the impact which the entry made and the questions it provoked (Matt. 21:4-5,9-11). Luke stresses the self-evident nature of the event: if the disciples did not cry out, the very stones would have done so! (Luke 19:39-40). John notes how the disciples came to understand Jesus' entry more clearly after his resurrection and ascension than they did at the time (John 12:16).

The coming of the King

Mark's presentation of the triumphal entry emphasizes that this King comes not only visibly but in reality. The heavenly meaning behind the earthly story becomes clear. Both the humility of a king riding on a donkey and the glory of his triumph are keynotes in his account. The reality of Jesus' spiritual kingdom grips us as he enters Jerusalem. The true nature of his kingship is to be seen even in the manner of his arrival. Mark underscores the fact that Jesus is a different kind of Messiah from that of popular expectation. He shows the link between one who is both suffering Servant and King of peace. He majors not only on the visible aspect of the kingly entry but on its inner intent as well.

Mark tells the story simply, sparingly, graphically. His words call for comment, for he himself gives little. It is like a parable from which the inner message must be teased out. Some details Mark omits, some he enlarges upon. There is a restrained vividness in his account. There is a hiddenness amid the clarity. Mark makes his own contribution to the story of Jesus, the royal King:

> As they approached Jerusalem and came to Bethphage and Bethany at the Mount of Olives, Jesus sent two of his disciples, saying to them, 'Go to the village ahead of you, and just as you enter it, you will find a colt tied there, which no one has ever ridden. Untie it and bring it here. If anyone asks you, "Why are you doing this?" tell him, "The Lord needs it and will send it back here shortly." '
>
> They went and found a colt outside in the street, tied at a doorway. As they untied it, some people standing there asked, 'What are you doing, untying that colt?' They answered as Jesus had told them to, and the people let them go. When they brought the colt to Jesus and threw their cloaks over it, he sat on it. Many people spread their cloaks on the road, while others spread branches they had cut in the fields. Those who went ahead and those who followed shouted,
>
> 'Hosanna!'
>
> 'Blessed is he who comes in the name of the Lord!'
>
> 'Blessed is the coming kingdom of our father David!'
>
> 'Hosanna in the highest!'
>
> Jesus entered Jerusalem and went to the temple. He looked around at everything, but since it was already late, he went out to Bethany with the Twelve (Mark 11:1-11).

Mark, with Luke, omits the quotation from Zechariah given in Matthew, but Mark develops the prophetic background in his own way. He, even more than Luke, majors on the donkey being untied and brought to Jesus (Mark 11:4-5) — a feature entirely omitted by Matthew. This recalls another Old Testament prophecy, Jacob's blessing of his sons:

> The sceptre will not depart from Judah,
>   nor the ruler's staff from between his feet,
> until he comes to whom it belongs
>   and the obedience of the nations is his.
> He will tether his donkey to a vine,
>   his colt to the choicest branch;
> he will wash his garments in wine,
>   his robes in the blood of grapes.
> His eyes will be darker than wine,
>   his teeth whiter than milk
>
> (Gen. 49:10-11).

The kingdom of David

The one phrase which is found only in Mark is the crowd's chanting comment on Psalm 118:25-26: 'Blessed is the coming kingdom of our father David!' (Mark 11:10). Matthew speaks of Jesus being acclaimed as the 'Son of David' and the one who 'comes in the name of the Lord' (Matt. 21:9). Luke records the use of the expression, 'the king who comes in the name of the Lord' (Luke 19:38), but Mark refers specifically to 'the coming kingdom of ... David'. This was the true significance of this occasion. Jesus was revealing his mission in terms of the true Messiah from the line of David. The crowd may not have realized the implications of what they were shouting out, but they were now witnessing the fulfilment of these words. There had been a time for careful instruction in which the Son of Man was revealed as Jehovah's suffering Servant. Now was the occasion for premeditated action: the Messiah was revealed as Jehovah's royal King, claiming a throne of salvation and establishing a kingdom of peace. Jesus was not the political Messiah the crowds longed for, but a spiritual Messiah establishing God's kingdom. 'Christ executeth the office of a king, in subduing us to himself, in ruling and defending us, and in restraining and conquering all his and our enemies' (*Shorter Catechism*, 26).

The King arrives in his capital

As we have already seen, Mark's account of Jesus' entry into Jerusalem is both restrained and emphatic. Compared with Matthew and Luke, he ends in a low-key fashion. Indeed, Matthew and Luke, all along, give the impression that the triumphal entry was a much larger-scale event than does Mark. Matthew speaks of 'a very large crowd' (Matt. 21:8) and Luke of 'the whole crowd of disciples' (Luke 19:37), while Mark simply uses the words 'many people' (Mark 11:8). Luke describes an animated debate between the Pharisees and Jesus about his disciples' behaviour (Luke 19:38-44). Matthew claims that the whole of Jerusalem was stirred by the man riding on the donkey whom they recognized as 'Jesus, the prophet from Nazareth in Galilee' (Matt. 21:10-11). Mark mentions none of these details.

Both Matthew and Luke give the next significant event as Jesus' cleansing of the temple. Mark, however, depicts Jesus, on his arrival in Jerusalem, as going into the temple, looking round at everything and then, because it was late, going out to Bethany with the Twelve (Mark 11:11). There is in fact no conflict between the Gospel writers. It is simply that Mark is showing that the King, having come to his capital, quietly overviews the scene and prepares for the next stage in his conquest. The royal King, having completed the first stage in his work, prepares for the second, as priestly King. It is not so much anti-climax as a lull before the storm.

The nature of Christ's kingdom

I remember talking to a man who had a drink problem. It had ruined his own life and was steadily wrecking his marriage and home. He would go to Alcoholics Anonymous and try them again. He had a friend who had done so. It had not worked, but eventually his friend had become a Christian and that had solved the problem. What did I think? Should he become a Christian? I told him that I believed God could solve his problem, but that there were two issues here — his drink problem and his sin problem. He must not simply fabricate becoming a Christian to have his drink problem solved. To become a Christian, he must recognize the equally enslaving and even greater sin problem he had, repent of his sin and receive Christ as Saviour. But the two issues must be kept separate. I shall never forget his honest, yet sad, reply. Concerning becoming a Christian he said, 'Ah! yes, I know, you have to have that in mind.'

Jesus entered Jerusalem, in the way that he did, so that people might have clearly in mind who he was and why he came. Angling for their acceptance of him on a political basis or playing on their emotions were alike out of the question. He had spent time teaching his followers that he must suffer and die. Now he publicly discloses the nature of his kingdom. It is not as activist, or even reformer, that he establishes his rule, but gently, as peace-maker and bringer of salvation. Then again, that salvation is not from Roman tyranny, nor even from human disaster, but from the dominion of sin. The spectacle of a fully grown man on an undersized donkey laying claim meekly

to a kingdom of peace, as foretold by the prophets, underlines
the truth that we come into Jesus' kingdom on his terms alone.

> Ride on! Ride on in majesty!
> Hark! All the tribes 'Hosanna!' cry;
> O Saviour meek, pursue thy road,
> With palms and scattered garments strewed.
>
> Ride on! Ride on in majesty!
> In lowly pomp ride on to die;
> O Christ, thy triumphs now begin
> O'er captive death and conquered sin.
>
> Ride on! Ride on in majesty!
> The winged squadrons of the sky
> Look down with sad and wondering eyes
> To see the approaching sacrifice.
>
> Ride on! Ride on in majesty!
> Thy last and fiercest strife is nigh;
> The Father on his sapphire throne
> Awaits his own anointed Son.
>
> Ride on! Ride on in majesty!
> In lowly pomp ride on to die;
> Bow thy meek head to mortal pain,
> Then take, O God, thy power, and reign.
>   (Henry Hart Milman, 1791-1868).

The priestly King cleanses the temple

The cursing of the fig tree and the cleansing of the temple are
acted parables of Jesus the priestly King. The King not only

lays claim to the throne, but cleanses the people over whom he rules. These are acts of royal judgement.

Two acts of judgement

The cursing of the fig tree portrays God's judgement on Israel. Few incidents in Jesus' life have received such a bad press as this one. Is the human Jesus so irritated, when hungry and finding no figs to satisfy his appetite, that, in a fit of pique, he curses an inanimate tree? Even worse, does he do so, when any reasonable person would know that it was not the season for figs? No, rather, Jesus the Messiah, not finding on the tree those early figs normally present at that time of year, proclaims a symbolic judgement on it. This symbolic judgement anticipates the real judgement which will fall on Israel. The nation's unique privileges from God have not resulted in fruit for God. We can have all the privileges of promise but lack the practical signs of fulfilment in our lives.

The cleansing of the temple declares judgement on a people where there is religion but no reality. It was the extortion practised by the money-changers within the temple court that so angered Jesus and made him act as he did. It was their devaluing of covenant principles, their exorbitant charges for money-changing and their obsession with gain that disturbed him so deeply. They were turning the house of God into a den of robbers. Their religion was hollow, shoddy, superficial and unreal. Righteous indignation, not a fit of bad temper, moved Jesus to act in judgement.

Mark shows that Jesus' response to this is not only negative but positive in its effects. It is not simply a judgemental act whereby sin is exposed, but also a redemptive one by which righteousness is introduced. Both these episodes, according to Mark, speak of the replacement of the old by the new.

The interweaving of the two events

Only Matthew and Mark record both these incidents. Matthew records them in order: the clearing of the temple first and the cursing of the fig tree second (Matt. 21:12-17,18-22). Mark interlocks both events. He introduces Christ's words of judgement on the tree as the disciples leave Bethany for Jerusalem, goes on to describe his cleansing of the temple and then, presumably on the next morning, shows Jesus returning to the withered tree:

> The next day as they were leaving Bethany, Jesus was hungry. Seeing in the distance a fig tree in leaf, he went to find out if it had any fruit. When he reached it, he found nothing but leaves, because it was not the season for figs. Then he said to the tree, 'May no one ever eat fruit from you again.' And his disciples heard him say it.
>
> On reaching Jerusalem, Jesus entered the temple area and began driving out those who were buying and selling there. He overturned the tables of the money-changers and the benches of those selling doves, and would not allow anyone to carry merchandise through the temple courts. And as he taught them, he said, 'Is it not written:
>
>> "My house will be called
>> a house of prayer for all nations?"
>
> But you have made it a den of robbers.
>
> The chief priests and the teachers of the law heard this and began looking for a way to kill him, for they feared him, because the whole crowd was amazed at his teaching.

When evening came, they went out of the city.

In the morning, as they went along, they saw the fig tree withered from the roots. Peter remembered and said to Jesus, 'Rabbi, look! The fig tree you cursed has withered!'

'Have faith in God,' Jesus answered. 'I tell you the truth, if anyone says to this mountain, "Go, throw yourself into the sea," and does not doubt in his heart but believes that what he says will happen, it will be done for him. Therefore I tell you, whatever you ask for in prayer, believe that you have received it, and it will be yours. And when you stand praying, if you hold anything against anyone, forgive him, so that your Father in heaven may forgive you your sins' (Mark 11:12-25).

By combining the two accounts in this way Mark is saying that both events are about the same thing. They are both pointing to judgement. As Joseph explained to Pharaoh, his two dreams — on cattle and corn — are really one and the same message. The double format emphasizes the fulfilment as imminent: there is an urgency about the whole matter. The judge stands at the door: 'The dreams of Pharaoh are one and the same. God has revealed to Pharaoh what he is about to do... The reason the dream was given to Pharaoh in two forms is that the matter has been firmly decided by God, and God will do it soon' (Gen. 41:25,32).

A new beginning

Both events speak of a decisive, judgemental act by the Messianic priest in which the old past is swept away and a new order is established. Messianic cleansing has abiding consequences. Jesus' enemies will be completely thwarted and a 'new' Israel will rise from the ashes of the old.

In the cleansing of the temple, Mark also mentions that Jesus bars any further traffic of merchandise through the temple court. Both Matthew and Luke omit this detail (Mark 11:15-16; cf. Matt. 21:12; Luke 19:45). Mark is showing that true cleansing means not just the removal of sin but the destruction of its source as well. A compromising religion, which flirts with the world, simply will not do. The break between old and new must be complete. True cleansing brings not just an end of old, false religion but the beginning of new, genuine faith.

In the same incident Mark alone includes, in Jesus' words, the full quotation from Isaiah, showing that the covenant is ultimately for the Gentile nations as well as for God's ancient people, Israel. The branches were broken off from Israel so that the Gentiles might be grafted in: 'My house will be called a house of prayer for all nations' (Mark 11:17; cf. Isa. 56:7).

The positive aspect — a living faith in God

Mark's account of the cursing of the fig tree is more detailed than Matthew's. Matthew mentions the disciples' question about the speedy withering of the tree (Matt. 21:20). Mark notes Peter's surprised statement to the same effect (Mark 11:21). Matthew includes among Jesus' words, in the ensuing discussion about faith, the fact that true faith shows itself in believing prayer (Matt. 21:21-22). Mark adds to this Jesus' comment that faith is evident not only in believing prayer but also in forgiving love (Mark 11:25); it affects not only communication with God but also relationship with one's fellow-man. True cleansing transforms both past and future before God and man. It has a positive as well as a negative side and a divine and a human interface. According to Mark, the priestly King saves and sanctifies, delivers and directs, liberates and leads his people. 'Christ executeth the office of a priest, in his once offering up of himself a sacrifice to satisfy divine justice, and reconcile us to God, and in making continual intercession for us' (*Shorter Catechism,* 25).

In the great missionary-statesman Hudson Taylor we have an example of the kind of faith which Jesus talks about in this passage. What was the secret of this man's effectiveness? What was the key to his biblical godliness? It was his faith, or rather, his *perception* of what true faith is. For Hudson Taylor faith involved cleansing, not just in deed but in intention as well; not just the removal of the old nature, but its replacement by the new; not just the grace of justification but the evidence of sanctification. Hudson Taylor rendered 'Have faith in God' (Mark 11:22) as 'Hold God's faithfulness'. His own words best express his view of faith: 'The verb translated "hold" is similarly rendered in Matthew 21:26, "All hold John as a prophet". In the corresponding passage in Mark 11:32, it is rendered "count"; and in Luke 20:6, a different Greek word is used which well illustrates the meaning, "They be persuaded that John was a prophet". Let us see that in theory we *hold* that God is faithful; that in daily life we *count* upon it; and that at all times and under all circumstances we are fully *persuaded* of this blessed truth.'

Hudson Taylor's faith in Jesus Christ was like that. It involved actively believing God's faithfulness in salvation, practically counting upon it daily and experimentally being persuaded of it whatever the circumstances. There was a positive as well as a negative side to the cleansing of Hudson Taylor's sins as a lad of seventeen. This cleansing led to a life of future righteousness. Has it done so with us?

The prophetic King silences the opposition

We now move on to the debates of Jesus with the religious leaders. These are the spoken parables of Jesus the prophetic

King. Here Jesus moves from actions to words. Words now supplement the earlier actions of the triumphal entry, the cursing of the fig tree and the cleansing of the temple. Jesus presses home his claims to kingship, not simply in symbolic deeds, but with answers, explanation and instruction.

There is progression as well. The momentum of the story has quickened; the drama moves speedily to its climax. Jesus comes and lays claim to the kingdom in his triumphal entry. This is the act of a royal King. Jesus next cleanses the house of Levi in the cursing of the fig tree and the cleansing of the temple. This is the work of a priestly King. Jesus now conquers by his kingship all who oppose him. It is the word of a prophetic King. It is a final word too, closing the debate, silencing all talk, quelling all opposition — the King in complete control of his kingdom. Finality marks that royal conquest.

The order of events

There is a strong similarity in this respect between Matthew, Mark and Luke. All three evangelists present the following events in the same order: the questioning of Jesus' authority by the religious leaders; the parable of the tenants; the question about paying taxes to Caesar; the debate with the Sadducees over marriage and the resurrection; and Jesus' question to them over whose son is the Christ. Matthew and Mark add the lawyer's query as to which is the greatest commandment. Mark and Luke close with the account of the widow's offering while Matthew concludes with seven woes pronounced against the religious teachers of the day (See the table opposite for a comparison of the three accounts.)

The opposition silenced

The context is an ongoing debate between the religious leaders and Jesus. The chief priests, teachers of the law, Pharisees,

	Matthew	**Mark**	**Luke**
Authority of Jesus questioned	21:23-27	11:27-33	20:1-8
Parable of two sons	21:28-32		
Parable of tenants	21:33-46	12:1-12	20:9-19
Parable of wedding banquet	22:1-14		
Paying taxes to Caesar	22:15-22	12:13-17	20:20-26
Marriage and resurrection	22:23-33	12:18-27	20:27-40
Which is greatest commandment?	22:34-40	12:28-34	
Whose son is Christ?	22:41-46	12:35-40	20:41-47
Seven woes	23:1-36		
Widow's offering		12:41-44	21:1-4

Herodians and Sadducees try to trap Jesus with their words and questions on abstruse and difficult points. Jesus clearly aims at the religious leaders in his parable of the tenants. All three evangelists stress how the religious leaders realized this and plotted Jesus' death. They were only prevented from taking further action by their fear of the people (Matt. 21:46; Mark 12:12; Luke 20:19).

Jesus handles all their questions with devastating precision, and then poses to them a question from Scripture which, if they attempt to answer it, will affirm out of their own lips that Jesus is indeed the Messiah. Jesus thus decisively silences further verbal attack: 'No one could say a word in reply and from that day on no one dared to ask him any more questions' (Matt. 22:46). 'And from then on no one dared ask him any more questions' (Mark 12:34). 'And no one dared to ask him any more questions' (Luke 20:40). The Lord Jesus is in complete control of the situation. All opposition has been dealt with. Jesus, the Messiah, not only comes visibly and cleanses effectively, but conquers finally. Silence ensues. There is nothing more to be said.

In these debates with the religious leaders Mark stresses the finality of Jesus' victory. The chief priests, teachers of the law and elders are, literally, dumbfounded as Jesus counter-questions them about John the Baptist's authority (Mark 11:31-33). The Sadducees are shown to be not only 'in error' of the Scriptures and God's power, but 'badly mistaken' as well (Mark 12:24,27).

Matthew notes how Jesus silenced the opposition after he put the question: 'Whose son is the Christ?' (Matt. 22:46). Luke places a similar comment at the close of the discussion with the Sadducees (Luke 20:39) and Mark after the debate with the teacher of the law on the greatest commandment (Mark 12:34).

A gracious victory

Mark's account of the question by the teacher of the law is fuller than that of Matthew. Mark quotes in full the *'Shema'*, the daily credo repeated by the Jew from Deuteronomy 6:4-5 about loving the Lord God with all one's being. Mark notes the teacher's admiration of Jesus' reply to the Sadducees, his warm reaction to Jesus' answer to his own question and Jesus' encouraging response to that reaction:

> One of the teachers of the law came and heard them debating. Noticing that Jesus had given them a good answer, he asked him, 'Of all the commandments, which is the most important?'
>
> 'The most important one,' answered Jesus, 'is this: "Hear, O Israel, the Lord our God, the Lord is one. Love the Lord your God with all your heart and with all your soul and with all your mind and with all your strength." The second is this: "Love your neighbour as yourself." There is no commandment greater than these.'
>
> 'Well said, teacher,' the man replied. 'You are right in saying that God is one and there is no other but him. To love him with all your heart, with all your understanding and with all your strength, and to love your neighbour as yourself is more important than all burnt offerings and sacrifices.'
>
> When Jesus saw that he had answered wisely, he said to him, 'You are not far from the kingdom of God.' And from then on no one dared ask him any more questions (Mark 12:28-34).

Mark is saying that Jesus as King is conquering not only with finality but in grace as well. Jesus is not only winning the argument; he is winning the man. The kind of victory evident through Jesus' debating skills with the religious teachers not only silences the opposition of enemies; it encourages the allegiance of those who will become friends. There is a positive as well as a negative side to the conquest. This is Mark's particular contribution on the issue of these debates.

This is what makes the sovereignty of God in Christ so dynamic. It is not the blind, fatalistic will of a capricious despot who imposes upon man a supremacy which man takes or leaves but can do little about. It is rather the loving care of a Father, who not only destroys all opposition but brings willing obedience to a sovereignty which seeks our highest good and well-being.

The graciousness of the rule of the kingdom is stressed throughout Mark. The disciples are called to become fishers of men (1:17). The paralysed man is not only healed but his sins are forgiven (2: 5). Those who leave all to follow Jesus are his family, his mother and brothers (3:35). Jairus must not fear, only believe (5:36). Frightened followers in the storm are to recognize Jesus and relinquish anxiety (6:50). Little children are encouraged to come to Jesus, for to such as these belongs to the kingdom of God (10:14). The King comes not only conquering with finality but in gracious sovereignty. Christ as King brings righteousness.

'Christ executeth the office of a prophet, in revealing to us by his Word and Spirit the will of God for our salvation' (*Shorter Catechism,* 24).

The need for a right view of God

Islamic fundamentalism is much in the news today. Islam has replaced Communism as a world-dominating force. It is the cause of bloodshed in the Middle East and elsewhere. It savages the Christian church in persecution. For years, the gospel made little inroads into Islamic nations. Generations of missionaries worked tirelessly there but with little or no tangible results. Now the situation has changed. In the Arab world, both in the Middle East and Africa, there have been converts to Christ. There is a thriving Christian church in Baghdad, which has recently called an Egyptian pastor. Muslim young people, disenchanted with Islam, are seeking alternative answers in Christianity. Interest in the Scriptures and their life-giving message grows. Its Christ-centred plan of salvation from Old to New Testament is increasingly being seen as both the true foundation and hope for those formerly under Islamic domination.

What is the nature of this glorious change brought about by the Spirit of God? It is, essentially, that those who formerly adhered to a fatalism that maintained that there is one god, Allah, and that Mohammed is his prophet, are now discovering in the true and living God a sovereignty, just as absolute as that of Allah, but full of grace and hope. As God gently draws these people to himself, the Bible replaces the Koran, and its life-giving message displaces blind ritualism. Christ's is a warm, inviting sovereignty, which hates the sin, draws the sinner to himself in love and yet maintains the absoluteness of his lordship.

Many today outside Islam have a mistaken view of God. They bear a grudge against him for some devastating distress in life. They depict him as being on the rim of the world, blandly disinterested in human distress, or mechanically handing out weal or woe. Their god is Allah, not Jehovah. They need to see the sovereignty of the true God, the King who, in Christ, brings a rule of grace and sovereignty of hope. Mark, in Jesus' triumphant entry to Jerusalem, in the cursing of the fig tree, in the cleansing of the temple and in Christ's debates with the religious leaders, presents such a King. Jesus comes as a royal King, cleanses as a priestly King and conquers as a prophetic King. He is the Christ, the Son of the living God, chosen and beloved. To him we must listen. Does this majestic King rule your life today? Has he brought you into submission to himself, cleansed you from sin, revealed himself to you by his Word and Spirit?

Join all the glorious names
Of wisdom, love and power,
That ever mortals knew,
That angels ever bore:
All are too mean to speak his worth,
Too mean to set my Saviour forth.

Great Prophet of my God,
My tongue would bless thy name;
By thee the joyful news
Of our salvation came,
The joyful news of sins forgiven,
Of hell subdued, and peace with heaven.

Jesus, my great High Priest,
Offered his blood and died;
My guilty conscience seeks
No sacrifice beside:
His powerful blood did once atone,
And now it pleads before the throne.

My dear Almighty Lord,
My Conqueror and my King,
Thy sceptre and thy sword,
Thy reigning grace, I sing:
Thine is the power: behold, I sit
In willing bonds before thy feet.

Now let my soul arise,
And tread the tempter down:
My Captain leads me forth
To conquest and a crown:
A feeble saint shall win the day,
Though death and hell obstruct the way.

Should all the hosts of death,
And powers of hell unknown,
Put their most dreadful forms
Of rage and mischief on,
I shall be safe; for Christ displays
Superior power and guardian grace.

(Isaac Watts, 1674-1748)

7.
Sacrificial Saviour

Most biographies tell their story stressing the importance of individual events in the person's life. Birth and upbringing receive some consideration. Education and formative influences are given their place. Career development and achievements gain most space. Personal life is not forgotten. Overall assessment is a necessary ingredient. Death is mentioned only briefly, a sad anti-climax to all that has gone before.

How different is the approach of the Gospel writers! They too give some details of Jesus' life, although his first thirty years are passed over in virtual silence. Within the three years of Jesus' public ministry an inordinate amount of space is given by all four evangelists to his death and the events immediately before and after it. The time schedule for this close coverage is not of months and weeks but of days and hours. Mark is particularly noticeable in this. Although no details are given of Jesus' birth, his death is reported intensively. Far from being a mere historical addendum, a sad but necessary anti-climax to his life, the death of Jesus is the crowning glory of Mark's Gospel. All the themes he has previously been weaving come together in a patterned way in that death.

All the Gospel writers report the events of that last week of Jesus' life: the Last Supper, Gethsemane, the betrayal by Judas, the arrest, the arraignment before the Sanhedrin, Peter's denial, the trial before Pilate, the crucifixion, death and burial. There is a remarkable similarity in the records of these events in Matthew, Mark and Luke. Mark's vivid touches and graphic detail are here too in the account of Jesus' death, but little is exclusive to Mark: just one intriguing detail — the sight of a young man virtually naked! 'Then everyone deserted him and fled. A young man, wearing nothing but a linen garment, was following Jesus. When they seized him, he fled naked, leaving his garment behind' (Mark 14:50-52).

Who was this young man? Many suggest it was Mark himself. The Last Supper may have been held at his home in Jerusalem, and following that, roused from his sleep, he was present at Jesus' arrest later that evening. In the fracas surrounding Jesus' arrest he runs off, his garment left behind. Mark mentions this immediately after noting that all Jesus' friends had fled in desertion.

Peter is there too in Mark's narrative, following Jesus at a distance right into the courtyard of the high priest; warming himself at the fire as Jesus faced the Sanhedrin; denying his Lord before one of the servant girls of the high priest; hearing the cock crow a second time, and then breaking down and sobbing. Peter would never forget those things. They were etched for ever on his conscience.

As Jesus predicts Peter's denial, Mark recalls more than the other writers the vehemence of Peter's insistence, using a word occurring only here in the New Testament: 'But Peter insisted emphatically [*'ekperissos'*], "Even if I have to die with you, I will never disown you." And all the others did the same' (Mark 14:31). It is as though Peter is confessing to his shame through this Gospel of Mark how he, even more than the others, pledged his allegiance.

In the trauma of Gethsemane, Mark alone records that Jesus' question is addressed, not just to Peter, but to Simon Peter, as though drawing attention to the fact that the old nature was still there: 'Then he returned to his disciples and found them sleeping. "Simon," he said to Peter, "are you asleep? Could you not keep watch for one hour? Watch and pray so that you will not fall into temptation. The spirit is willing, but the body is weak" ' (Mark 14:37-38).

All the Gospel writers record Peter's denials of knowing Jesus with detail that might well have come from Peter's own lips: the questions put to him by the girl; the intensity with which she scrutinized Peter; the affirmations and oaths that accompanied his subsequent denials. Yet Mark adds further details. He alone describes this girl as 'one of the servant girls of the high priest' (Mark 14:66). He records the emphatic negations in Peter's words: 'I don't know or understand what you're talking about... I don't know this man you're talking about' (Mark 14:68,71). This kind of extra detail is one reason why many infer that Peter himself was Mark's main oral source for the writing of his Gospel.

Mark gathers up all the threads of Jesus' life and ministry and completes them in the story of his death in a personal and vivid way. Jesus as Son of God, mentioned at the outset of the Gospel, as Son of Man, woven into the fabric of the Gospel, fulfils his ministry in his death as sacrificial Saviour. Jesus stands before Caiaphas arraigned as the condemned Messiah for every Jew to see. Jesus appears before Pilate as a crucified King for every Roman to view. Jesus hangs on the cross before an unnamed centurion as the confessed Son of God for all the world to ponder. Jesus dies as Saviour for every man to encounter. Mark makes all mankind face the Christ who sacrifices his life to ransom guilty sinners. Have you faced up to the demands of the sacrificial Saviour?

Condemned Messiah

A travesty of justice

Jesus' arraignment before the Sanhedrin was a charade, a misnomer for a trial:

> They took Jesus to the high priest, and all the chief priests, elders and teachers of the law came together. Peter followed him at a distance, right into the court-yard of the high priest. There he sat with the guards and warmed himself at the fire.
>
> The chief priests and the whole Sanhedrin were look-ing for evidence against Jesus so that they could put him to death, but they did not find any. Many testified falsely against him, but their statements did not agree.
>
> Then some stood up and gave this false testimony against him: 'We heard him say, "I will destroy this man-made temple and in three days will build another, not made by man." ' Yet even then their testimony did not agree.
>
> Then the high priest stood up before them and asked Jesus, 'Are you not going to answer? What is this testi-mony that these men are bringing against you?' But Jesus remained silent and gave no answer.
>
> Again the high priest asked him, 'Are you the Christ, the Son of the Blessed One?'
>
> 'I am,' said Jesus. 'And you will see the Son of Man sitting at the right hand of the Mighty One and coming on the clouds of heaven.'
>
> The high priest tore his clothes. 'Why do we need any more witnesses?' he asked. 'You have heard the blas-phemy. What do you think?'

They all condemned him as worthy of death. Then
some began to spit at him; they blindfolded him, struck
him with their fists, and said, 'Prophesy!' And the guards
took him and beat him (Mark 14:53-65).

Caiaphas was the leading participant. He was high priest
from A.D. 18 to 37. He was the son-in-law of Annas and
worked in close co-operation with him. Caiaphas was wily,
intent on getting his own way, by hook or by crook. We see
this from his treatment of Jesus and later of Peter and John,
who also appeared before the Sanhedrin. His unease about
trying Jesus at the time of an important Jewish festival and his
enigmatic statement about the expediency of one man dying
for the people show him in his true colours. Josephus, the
Jewish historian, who had once been a Pharisee, confirms that
Caiaphas was a shady character. Caiaphas led the plot to destroy Jesus.

As the chief Jewish court, consisting of chief priests, elders
and teachers of the law, the Sanhedrin gave judgement within
the temple precinct. They sat in a semi-circle and heard witnesses' testimony. Those testimonies had to agree. When giving verdicts on capital offences, the Sanhedrin did so individually from the youngest to the eldest. For the death penalty,
there had to be a lapse overnight for reconsideration of the
judgement. They were forbidden to meet at night or during a
festival time. Strict rules governed their procedure.

Clearly these rules were broken at Jesus' trial. They met at
Caiaphas' home, not in the temple. It was close to the Passover and they met under cover of darkness, not in daylight.
The whole proceedings were rushed. Testimony did not agree.
Immediate sentence of death was given with no opportunity
for reconsideration. Individual verdicts were not taken. The
matter was dispatched forthwith and Jesus was condemned to
death for 'blasphemously' claiming to be Messiah. It was all

over hastily and illegally before the cock crowed heralding the dawn.

Mark underlines the façade connected with the proceedings. He gives the most detail of the accusations against Jesus and stresses the disagreements in the statements made against him (Mark 14:55-59; cf. Matt. 26:59-61). But it is not the infringement of legal forms on which Mark majors. Rather, it is the leaders' intention not to reach a just verdict but to convict Jesus of a capital crime that Mark emphasizes. This has been their intention for quite some time and now it reaches a climax (Mark 3:6; 11:18; 12:12; 14:1-2,55). Mark wants us to realize that this was no fair trial by any standard at all.

Jesus revealed as Messiah

Caiaphas' question, using the words 'Christ'and 'Son of the Blessed One' (Mark 14:61; cf. Luke 22:66,70), asked Jesus whether or not he was the 'Messiah'. The sense in which Caiaphas used the title made it plain that he was speaking of the Messiah's relationship with God. In Mark, Jesus' reply to Caiaphas was crystal clear: ' "Are you the Christ, the Son of the Blessed One?" "I am," said Jesus. "And you will see the Son of Man sitting at the right hand of the Mighty One and coming on the clouds of heaven" ' (Mark 14:61-62). To the question, 'Are you the Messiah?', Jesus not only replies, 'Yes', but goes on to define that affirmation from Old Testament prophecies. Jesus affirms that he is the Son of God who sits at God's right hand, the great King-Priest predicted by David (Ps. 110:1). Jesus asserts that he is the Son of Man who comes in the clouds of heaven, the great Mediator and Judge foretold by Daniel (Dan. 7:13). It could not have been a clearer testimony. This was why Caiaphas symbolically tore his clothes and denied the need for further witnesses. They had enough evidence now to condemn Jesus to death for blasphemy.

Matthew gives Jesus' reply as 'Yes', but in a defined way. He was indeed the Messiah, the Son of God, just as the high priest's question inferred (Matt. 26:63-64).

Luke gives Jesus' reply, first as 'Yes' by implication and then as 'Yes' in a guarded fashion. He was in fact telling them, but they were only interested in his answer for the sake of entrapping him (Luke 22:66-70).

Mark's bold 'I am' is yet more emphatic than Matthew or Luke in terms of its expression. All three evangelists refer to the coming of the Son of Man in judgement, but Jesus' reply according to Mark is the clearest and most challenging 'Yes' of all. It ruffles every feather in the Sanhedrin.

Jesus' openness is remarkable in view of his silence immediately beforehand. He has just refused to answer the charge that he would destroy the temple and build another. Now he claims publicly that he is the Messiah. It is even more remarkable, when we remember how that constantly, during his ministry, Jesus had commanded silence about his being the Messiah. Mark, especially among the evangelists, stresses this. Demons who want to make Jesus known are silenced (Mark 1:25,34; 3:11-12). Silence is enjoined after notable miracles (Mark 1:44; 5:43; 7:36; 8:26). Peter, who confessed Jesus as Messiah, must not make this known (Mark 8:30). Similar disclosures on the Mount of Transfiguration must remain secret (Mark 9:9). Jesus withdraws from the crowd on secret journeys and instructs his disciples privately on the subject of his suffering as Messiah (Mark 7:24; 8:30-31; 9:30-31;10:32-34). Now, facing the Jews in the most solemn and public of settings, Jesus throws silence to the wind and openly affirms that he is Messiah. What can this mean?

It means that Jesus has reached the end of his mission. *Now* is the time for a public disclosure of all that he has been teaching his disciples in private. Mark especially makes this clear. The time has come. The plan is ripe. The secret must now be divulged. All that Mark has been hinting at throughout his Gospel now becomes perfectly clear. Jesus is the Son of Man. He stands before Caiaphas, arraigned as the condemned Messiah, for every Jew to see. Can you see clearly who he is, and do his claims challenge you to the very core of your being?

While Caiaphas appears to be in command, all his craft and guile subside before the majestic assertion of Jesus that he is indeed the Messiah. The arraignment before Caiaphas is the climax of Mark's portrayal of Jesus the Son of Man. He is the Messiah, for all to see; the sacrificial Saviour who gives his life as a ransom for many.

Crucified King

As Mark focuses on the arraignment of Jesus before Caiaphas, he discloses him as the Messiah condemned by the Jews. As he highlights his trial before Pilate, he portrays him as the King of Israel crucified by the Romans. The sacrificial Saviour dies at the hands of wicked men according to the determinate counsel and foreknowledge of God. God's sovereignty and man's sin are exposed in the final act of Mark's drama. The Son of Man dies as condemned Messiah and as crucified King. Mark's story moves to its conclusion.

The trial before Pilate was certainly different from the arraignment before Caiaphas. The setting was probably the Fortress of Antonio, hard by the precincts of the temple in Jerusalem. An elevated stone platform was there where the procurator would ascend to give judgement. It was his prerogative to do so. He had his legal advisers for consultation but, unlike in the Sanhedrin, judgement was personal rather than corporate. Indictment of the accused was made first. Statement for the defence followed. Testimony of witnesses was given. The procurator would then interview the prisoner, consult his advisers and pass judgement. A. N. Sherwin-White, a specialist in Roman law, comments, 'In the hearing before Pilate, the Markan narrative fits the Roman framework well, considering that it was written with an entirely different purpose in mind.' On Pilate's shoulders alone rested ultimate responsibility for the judicial verdict on Jesus.

Uncertainty marks Pilate's behaviour throughout the proceedings with Jesus. He was procurator of the Roman province of Judea from A.D. 26 to 36. His track record with the Jews was anything but commendable. Early on he had antagonized them by attempting to set up Roman standards bearing the emperor's image in the holy city. Frustrated over that, he dedicated shields, bearing no image but only an inscription, in his own residence in Jerusalem. The Emperor Tiberius then ordered the shields to be set up in Rome instead. Josephus recalls how Pilate used money from the temple treasury to build an aqueduct in Jerusalem. Against this the Jews demonstrated in great numbers at festival time. Pilate sent in troops who slaughtered many. This made relations between Herod and Pilate frigid, to say the least. Finally, as a result of violence against the Samaritans, the procurator was recalled to Rome to answer for his harsh behaviour. Philo describes Pilate as 'inflexible, merciless and obstinate'; a man who repeatedly inflicted punishment without previous trial and committed ever so many acts of cruelty.

Pilate's dilemma

The case of Jesus of Nazareth was brought by the Jews before this man. What was Pilate to do? Amazed at Jesus' silence before his accusers, aware that no real case of sedition is involved, Pilate actually seems to have bartered with the Jews to release Jesus. The harder he tried, the worse things got. A way of escape presented itself. Two forms of amnesty existed under Roman law: *'abolitio'*, or acquittal of a prisoner not yet condemned, and *'indulgentia'*, or pardoning of one already condemned. He opted for the former but his plan misfired. Those wretched Jews cornered him and insisted on the release of the rebel Barabbas rather than Jesus of Nazareth. His hand was forced to crucify Jesus, the King of the Jews:

Very early in the morning, the chief priests, with the elders, the teachers of the law and the whole Sanhedrin, reached a decision. They bound Jesus, led him away and turned him over to Pilate.

'Are you the king of the Jews?' asked Pilate.

'Yes, it is as you say,' Jesus replied.

The chief priests accused him of many things. So again Pilate asked him, 'Aren't you going to answer? See how many things they are accusing you of.'

But Jesus still made no reply, and Pilate was amazed.

Now it was the custom at the Feast to release a prisoner whom the people requested. A man called Barabbas was in prison with the insurrectionists who had committed murder in the uprising. The crowd came up and asked Pilate to do for them what he usually did.

'Do you want me to release to you the king of the Jews?' asked Pilate, knowing it was out of envy that the chief priests had handed Jesus over to him. But the chief priests stirred up the crowd to have Pilate release Barabbas instead.

'What shall I do, then, with the one you call the king of the Jews?' Pilate asked them.

'Crucify him!' they shouted.

'Why? What crime has he committed?' asked Pilate.

But they shouted all the louder, 'Crucify him!'

Wanting to satisfy the crowd, Pilate released Barabbas to them. He had Jesus flogged, and handed him over to be crucified (Mark 15:1-15).

Jesus' reply

Jesus stands in the middle of all this, quietly supreme. To Pilate, Jesus' words are sparing and restrictive. Pilate is amazed. Jesus' behaviour seems preposterous to him. This Jew plays with death as though it were a game. The irony behind the whole thing is that Jesus seems more the judge and Pilate the prisoner than vice-versa.

' "Are you the King of the Jews?" asked Pilate. "Yes, it is as you say," Jesus replied' (Mark 15:2). The answer is in exactly the same form in Matthew, Mark and Luke (Matt. 27:11; Mark 15:2; Luke 23:3). While it could have meant, 'So you say,' in Aramaic idiom, it more probably meant 'Yes'. Jesus' answer is 'Yes', but in a defined way. A king he is, just as Pilate's question infers. But both Pilate and Jesus know that Jesus' brand of kingship is very different from that which the Jews stated in their accusation. Jesus was no political rebel. Otherwise, Pilate would have terminated the interview there and then and given judgement immediately. His Roman sense of justice would have required that. But Pilate did not terminate the interview; he continued to question Jesus. Jesus' reply to Caiaphas was forthright, supported by Old Testament Scripture regarding his Messianic role. Jesus' answer to Pilate was carefully worded, concerning his kingly office.

'The King of the Jews'

Mark pinpoints Pilate's dilemma and Jesus' reply as part of the climax of his Gospel. It is intriguing how the title 'King of the Jews' threads its way through Mark's account. Pilate's vital question and Jesus' searching reply are followed by varied Jewish accusations (Mark 15:2,3). Mark then records Pilate's suggestion that he release 'the king of the Jews' (Mark 15:9). This title forms the substance of Pilate's legal question (Mark 15:2) and is part of his appeal to the crowd (Mark

15:9-12). It is used in mockery by his soldiers (Mark 15:18) and is the designation adopted in the superscription on the cross (Mark 15:26). As the Jewish teachers ridicule the dying Jesus, they do so not only for his Messianic claims but for his kingly aspirations: 'Let this Christ, this King of Israel, come down now from the cross, that we may see and believe' (Mark 15:32).

The prominence Mark gives to the title 'King of the Jews' is significant. Jesus not only stands condemned as Messiah before Jewish eyes, but he stands indicted before a Gentile world as a 'spiritual' king. Here is the climax of Mark's Gospel. Jesus is not only the Jewish Messiah but also the universal King. Yet he is crucified — a crucified king for both Jewish and Roman eyes to see. He is both the 'Christ' and the 'King of Israel' (Mark 15:32). Words spoken by Pilate in scathing derision and by Jewish leaders in mocking scorn form the culmination of Mark's story.

The king revealed

Donald English, quoting from C. F. D. Moule, catches something of Mark's unique presentation when he writes, 'Jesus' silence, on an issue of life and death, amazes Pilate. Moule's comment sums up the situation well: The irony of the situation is overpowering: Jesus, who is, indeed, king of the Jews in a deeply spiritual sense, has refused to lead a spiritual uprising. Yet now condemned for blasphemy by the Jews because of his spiritual claims, he is accused by them also before Pilate for being precisely what he had disappointed the crowds by failing to be — a political insurgent. Jesus refused either to plead guilty or to defend himself. The silence of the suffering servant in Isaiah 53:7 again comes to mind. Pilate's attitude of "amazement" picks up a characteristic theme of Mark's Gospel, a sense which people have that more is going on than meets the eye.'

Mark's peculiar emphasis on a condemned Messiah before Jewry and on a crucified King before the Gentiles reinforces this sense that more is going on than meets the eye. The secrecy is peculiarly Mark's and so is the exposé. It is Mark's own fitting climax to his tale. The secret is finally and gloriously out. Jesus is both Messiah and Lord, Christ and King.

A young friend whom I knew always seemed to have had an interest in becoming a Christian. Brought up in a Christian home, he attended Sunday school, youth fellowship and was regular at church services. In that respect he was unlike Pilate, neither supercilious nor scornful. Again and again, he attempted to become a Christian but never succeeded — something was wrong. As his pastor, I was frightened that for him familiarity would breed contempt and that he would give up the whole matter in frustration. Sadly, I had seen that happen in other cases.

Eventually, he did come to faith and the reality of that profession continues to evidence itself. As I pondered the process of grace I realized this: while he was unlike Pilate in his openness and interest in Jesus, he was like Pilate in his failure to recognize and to take seriously the nature of Christ's kingship. The whole issue was viewed by him in terms only of human decision, not of submission of his will to the will of Christ the King. Like Pilate, his view of Christ's kingship was purely human. Matthew Henry says that 'The great change in conversion is wrought upon the will and consists of the resignation of that will to the will of Christ.' Mark reveals Jesus as the Son of Man, crucified as King for Jew and Gentile. He is a Messiah who meets our need and yet a King who commands our obedience. My young friend discovered this in becoming a Christian. Have we surrendered to the claims of Jesus the King? Mark's Gospel in particular poses that question.

Confessed Son

Jesus appears before Caiaphas as the condemned Messiah and before Pilate as the crucified King, the suffering Son of Man. Before a centurion standing at the cross, Jesus appears as the confessed Son of God, gloriously exalted even in death. Mark brings the Son of God and Son of Man motifs together in his story of the sacrificial Saviour:

> At the sixth hour darkness came over the whole land until the ninth hour. And at the ninth hour Jesus cried out in a loud voice, *'Eloi, Eloi, lama sabachthani?'* — which means, 'My God, my God, why have you forsaken me?'
> When some of those standing near heard this, they said, 'Listen, he's calling Elijah.'
> One man ran, filled a sponge with wine vinegar, put it on a stick, and offered it to Jesus to drink. 'Now leave him alone. Let's see if Elijah comes to take him down,' he said.
> With a loud cry, Jesus breathed his last.
> The curtain of the temple was torn in two from top to bottom. And when the centurion, who stood there in front of Jesus, heard his cry and saw how he died, he said, 'Surely this man was the Son of God!' (Mark 15:33-39).

The scene is very different from the two previous ones. It is neither the forbidding residence of the Jewish high priest, nor the Fortress of Antonio with its ordered rooms, but the hill of Golgotha outside Jerusalem. The person at the centre of the scene has changed too. It is neither sly Caiaphas, with his Jewish friends, nor sceptical Pilate, with his Roman advisers, but an unnamed centurion with his quaternion of soldiers, keeping official vigil at the execution of three felons. We learn about Caiaphas and Pilate both from the Scriptures and from secular literature. We know nothing of the centurion apart from what the Gospel writers have recorded. Was he a rough and gruff soldier coldly doing his duty, little interested in any religion, least of all that of the Jews? Or was he like the centurion whose servant Jesus had healed at Capernaum — kind to the Jews, respectful towards Jesus, an upright, interested man? We simply do not know.

A barrier removed

From the way Mark tells his story, however, we can and do learn some important things about the centurion. It is the actual moment of Jesus' death: 'With a loud cry, Jesus breathed his last' (Mark 15:37). At this, the heavy curtain in the temple is dramatically torn from top to bottom. Mark alone links this to the centurion's remarks. It is as though the tearing of that curtain is symbolic of what follows with that man. Just as that curtain admitted the high priest alone once a year into the inner sanctuary, but otherwise prevented access to Jews, and most certainly to Gentiles, so with Christ's death that barrier was removed. Roman centurions now had access to the inner presence of God through the Messiah too.

What impressed the centurion?

Mark notes what the centurion discovered and how he discovered it: 'And when the centurion, who stood there in front of Jesus, heard his cry and saw how he died, he said, "Surely this man was the Son of God!" ' (Mark 15:39). Mark claims that Jesus' cry and the manner of his death impressed the centurion. But to what cry does Mark refer? Was it that final cry of triumph, 'It is finished' (John 19:30), or that ultimate assertion before God, 'Father, into your hands I commit my spirit'? (Luke 23:46). Perhaps it refers to that earlier cry which Mark has just recorded: 'My God, my God, why have you forsaken me?' (Mark 15:34). If that were so, it would be intriguing: religious Jews around the cross missed the meaning of that cry; a Gentile centurion catches not only the drift of this cry, but of all of Jesus' words, especially this last, and confesses, 'Surely this man was the Son of God!' (Mark 15:39).

The centurion would have seen how other men died in crucifixion. He would know about the flies, the heat, the physical pain as the torn body sagged from the gibbet. Men hanging there cursed and vowed vengeance like the two thieves. Some reflected, confessed, even turned to God in the end, like the penitent thief. But none died like this man. None asked forgiveness for enemies, cried out his love to friends, offered hope to others and saw the whole sorry mess as God's plan. Jesus' cry and the way he died convinced a Gentile soldier of things lost on an audience of Jewish mockers, says Mark.

Matthew recalls the tearing of the temple curtain, a violent earthquake, tombs breaking open, the bodies of many holy people who had died being raised to life and appearing to many folk in Jerusalem (Matt. 27:51-53). Matthew then remarks that the centurion and those with him, on seeing the earthquake and all that had happened, were terrified and exclaimed, 'Surely he was the Son of God!' (Matt. 27:54).

Luke describes, at Jesus' death, three hours of darkness, the temple curtain torn in two, Jesus calling out in a loud voice, 'Father, into your hands I commit my spirit,' and then breathing his last (Luke 23:44-46). Luke tells us that the centurion, 'seeing what had happened, praised God and said, "Surely this was a righteous man" ' (Luke 23:47).

Mark mentions no earthquake, no darkness, no resurrected bodies. He recalls the severing of the temple curtain, then immediately describes the centurion's reaction. He specifically attributes the centurion's reaction, 'Surely this man was the Son of God!' to his hearing of Jesus' cry and to seeing how he died (Mark 15:38-39). For Mark these other extraordinary, even miraculous, details mentioned by Matthew and Luke are peripheral. What really impresses the centurion, according to Mark, even if the other factors contribute, is Jesus himself. That is the nub of Mark's presentation. That fits into the climax of his theme. Caiaphas the Jew and Pilate the Gentile make their sceptical comments. Now an unnamed Roman centurion makes a glorious statement. He is convinced — gloriously and fearfully convinced — by Jesus himself. Mark's climax is not about earthquakes, darkness, or resurrected saints, but about Jesus, Son of Man and Son of God.

How much of the truth did the centurion grasp?

But convinced of what? Can we really hold that the centurion regarded Jesus as the eternally begotten Son of God? Most commentators recoil from that interpretation. After all, 'the Son' could be taken as 'a son'. The centurion may simply have been claiming, within the limits of his own understanding, Jesus to be a deified hero, a divine man, or even simply a 'good' man. Luke's description 'a righteous man' would give a similar sense (Luke 23:47).

Calvin comments on this centurion: 'The centurion had not undergone such a change as to dedicate himself to God for the remainder of his life, but was only for a moment the herald of the divinity of Christ… Now when the centurion bestows on him the praise of righteousness, and pronounces him to be innocent, he likewise acknowledges him to be the Son of God; not that he understood distinctly how Christ was begotten by God the Father, but because he entertains no doubt that there is some divinity in him, and, convinced by proofs, holds it to be certain that Christ was not an ordinary man, but had been raised up by God.'

The Son is revealed

This is precisely Mark's purpose in recording the centurion's words. What Caiaphas angrily repudiates and Pilate scathingly dismisses, an unnamed Roman centurion begins to apprehend with amazement and conviction. Mark's Christ stands completely revealed. The Son of God at the start of Mark's story and the Son of Man throughout his tale is the condemned Messiah, crucified King and confessed Son, at the conclusion of the saga. And Jesus of Nazareth is supremely in his death the sacrificial Saviour of his people, Jew and Gentile alike.

I often wonder what happened to that centurion afterwards? Did he eventually become a Christian, or was the spectacle for ever lost on him? How we need to seek and instruct the modern equivalents of the Roman centurion around us to find, understand and love our Saviour — the eternally begotten Son of the eternal Father, our God and Saviour Jesus Christ! What do you, who read Mark's story, think of Jesus, condemned Messiah, crucified King, confessed Son? What impact does the death of this sacrificial Saviour make on you? Like Pilate, we each of us must answer that question: 'What then shall I do with Jesus, who is called Christ?' Mark forces that issue upon us.

> Jesus is standing in Pilate's hall—
> Friendless, forsaken, betrayed by all:
> Hearken! what meaneth the sudden call?
> What will you do with Jesus?
>
> *What will you do with Jesus?*
> *Neutral you cannot be;*

Someday your heart will be asking,
  'What will he do with me?'

Jesus is standing on trial still,
You can be false to him if you will,
You can be faithful through good or ill:
What will you do with Jesus?

Will you evade him, as Pilate tried?
Or will you choose him, whatever betide?
Vainly you struggle from him to hide:
What will you do with Jesus?

Will you, like Peter, your Lord deny?
Or will you scorn from his foes to fly,
Daring for Jesus to live or die?
What will you do with Jesus?

  'Jesus, I give thee my heart today!
  Jesus, I'll follow thee all the way,
  Gladly obeying thee!' Will you say,
  'This will I do with Jesus'?

                              (A. B. Simpson)

8.
Triumphant Lord

Most people love a happy ending. Whether it is a novel, play or film, a tragic finish always makes us feel disappointed. Even when we know that things will not turn out well, even if we have read the story or seen the film before and know the ending is unhappy, we experience that lump in the throat, a sense of loss, a desire to get away and forget the whole thing. An American television series used to carry a closing scene entitled 'Epilog'. There was usually a happy ending, the triumph of good over evil, and the 'Epilog' summed up the story and brought out the moral. Sometimes it was humorous, sometimes contrived, an ending tucked on that did not really fit the foregoing sequence. In those cases, it was almost worse than a sad ending, for it was artificial and detracted from the story.

As the Gospel writers present their final chapter on Jesus' resurrection, it is never like that. The suffering Saviour is also the triumphant Lord, but the link between Jesus' death and resurrection is neither contrived nor artificial. We never get the impression that we are stepping from a world of reality into fantasy, a happy ending merely added to take away the sting of the tragedy of Jesus' death. The story flows through naturally. There is a 'matter-of-fact' feel to that last chapter with all its extraordinary and miraculous detail, which makes it an integral, if amazing, part of the same sequence of events. A calm presentation of evidence is the keynote.

The last chapter brings hope, joy and purpose. But the data is given in the same way as before. Factual information is presented as evidence for the resurrection of Jesus from death. The account of Jesus as triumphant, risen Lord is a meaningful continuation, not a superficial epilogue, to the Gospel story.

Mark's account of the resurrection is much shorter than those of the other Gospel writers. There is not the same fulness as we find even in Matthew. Christ's appearances to the two journeying disciples and then to the eleven are mentioned in Mark, but with none of the exciting detail Luke gives. Christ's conversations with Mary Magdalene, Thomas and Peter, recorded by John, are absent from Mark. Yet, scant as Mark's details are, they are graphic and full of meaning. They carry their own message. They present, in short compass, stirring evidence which makes the resurrection a vital part of the story. For Mark Jesus is both sacrificial Saviour and triumphant Lord. Mark's final chapter is a natural continuation, not an abrupt epilogue, to his gospel story.

Continuation, not epilogue

Mark's story of the resurrection harks back to earlier features in his Gospel: 'He said to them, "The Son of Man is going to be betrayed into the hands of men. They will kill him, and after three days he will rise." But they did not understand what he meant and were afraid to ask him about it' (Mark 9:31-32).

Jesus' death and resurrection are two sides of the coin of his redemptive work. Mark makes this clear in the way he explains how Jesus the sacrificial Saviour becomes the triumphant Lord:

When the Sabbath was over, Mary Magdalene, Mary the mother of James, and Salome bought spices so that they might go to anoint Jesus' body. Very early on the first day of the week, just after sunrise, they were on their way to the tomb and they asked each other, 'Who will roll the stone away from the entrance of the tomb?'

But when they looked up, they saw that the stone, which was very large, had been rolled away. As they entered the tomb, they saw a young man dressed in a white robe sitting on the right side, and they were alarmed.

'Don't be alarmed,' he said. 'You are looking for Jesus the Nazarene, who was crucified. He has risen! He is not here. See the place where they laid him. But go, tell his disciples and Peter, "He is going ahead of you into Galilee. There you will see him, just as he told you." '

Trembling and bewildered, the women went out and fled from the tomb. They said nothing to anyone, because they were afraid (Mark 16:1-8).

The time

The chronological sequence of events is stressed in Mark's resurrection account. All the Gospel writers note this. They are concerned to indicate that Jesus rose the third day after death. Matthew states that it happened after the Sabbath, at dawn on the first day of the week (Matt. 28:1). Luke makes the point that it was 'very early' on the first day of the week when the women took the spices to anoint Jesus (Luke 23:56; 24:1). John says that 'it was still dark' early on the first day of the week when Mary Magdalene went to the tomb (John 20:1). Mark is equally precise. He combines the fact of completed Sabbath rest with their early purchase of spices on the first day and a very early arrival at the tomb. Mark alone mentions the buying of the spices: 'When the Sabbath was over, Mary Magdalene, Mary the mother of James and Salome bought spices so that they might go to anoint Jesus' body. Very early on the first day of the week, just after sunrise, they were on their way to the tomb' (Mark 16:1-2).

The place

Place plays a prominent role in Mark's presentation too. The Gospels refer to the empty tomb and to Galilee. Again, Mark's references are sparing but pointed. The stone which had been rolled to the mouth of the tomb is now an obstacle to their plans (Mark 15:46; 16:3). Mark alone mentions the stone as a specific 'problem'. Galilee, as a location, recalls words spoken by Jesus earlier in Mark's Gospel (Mark 14:28; 16:7). Nazareth, Jesus' home town, quoted in the young man's words at the end of Mark's story, echoes the acclamation of Jesus' divinity at the beginning (Mark 1:24; 16:6). Mark is pulling us back to the start of the story and confirming that the very person who rose was the Jesus who had been reared in Nazareth.

Mark is particularly emphasizing when and where the resurrection occurred. In addition, he stresses that the resurrection is not only a real event in space and time, but a predetermined one too. We are in the realm, not of make-believe, but of historical fact and fulfilled prophecy. W. L. Lane in his commentary on Mark's Gospel says, 'The resurrection of Jesus is an historical event. On a given date, in a defined place, the man Jesus, having been crucified and buried two days earlier, came forth from the tomb.'

The women

The women feature forcefully in the story here. They, not the disciples, are the first to experience the risen Jesus. Matthew records how Mary Magdalene and the other Mary go to look at the tomb. They meet an angel whose appearance is like lightning and whose clothes are white as snow. The angel tells the women of Jesus' rising and that the risen Jesus will meet them in Galilee. Hurrying away, afraid yet filled with joy, the women rush off to tell the disciples. Suddenly they meet Jesus, who encourages them not to be afraid but to tell the disciples to go to Galilee, where they will see him (Matt. 28:1-10).

Luke describes the women as entering the tomb to treat the body of Jesus with the spices. Not finding the body, they see two men in clothes gleaming like lightning. They tell the women that Jesus has risen and urge them to remember how Jesus had foretold this in Galilee. The women recall Jesus' words, return and tell the Eleven and all the others. The women concerned are Mary Magdalene, Joanna, Mary the mother of James and others with them. The apostles, however, do not believe the women (Luke 24:1-12).

John concentrates on Mary Magdalene who, waiting behind in the garden after she has told Peter and John, meets the risen Jesus, and then goes to the disciples with the news (John 20:1-18).

Mark's details are brief, factual and vivid. Mark is like a window through which we can see not only the women but their minds and feelings. Previously mentioned by name at the crucifixion of Jesus, now Salome joins the two Marys (Mark 15:40,47;16:1). They come to anoint the body of Jesus with perfumed spices, for they are afraid that decay may already have started (Mark 16:1). They have not the slightest inkling of Jesus' rising; they are concerned about his corpse. So for them the immediate problem, stressed by Mark alone, is the huge stone: 'Who will roll the stone away from the entrance of the tomb?' (Mark 16:3). The angel in Mark's account seems particularly to be seen through the women's eyes: 'a young man dressed in a white robe sitting on the right side' (Mark 16:5). The women take to their heels and run away 'alarmed', 'trembling', 'bewildered' and 'afraid' (Mark 16:5,8).

The young man

The young man and his words to the women stand out forcefully in Mark's Gospel. That Mark describes the messenger as
'a young man dressed in a white robe' and Matthew as 'an
angel of the Lord', whose 'appearance was like lightning, and
his clothes were white as snow', are distinctions that present
no real difficulty of interpretation (Mark 16:5; cf. Matt. 28:3).
The former may be the women's description, the latter that of
the terrified guards. The content of the angel's message is what
is important.

Matthew stresses the absence of Jesus' body, the fact that
the crucified Jesus had risen just as he said he would, the invitation to view the empty tomb and the command to tell the
disciples to go to Galilee where they would see the risen Lord
(Matt. 28:5-7). Luke emphasizes the absence of the body of
Jesus, the fact that Jesus had risen and the angel's encouragement to remember Jesus' teaching that 'The Son of Man must
be delivered into the hands of sinful men, be crucified and on
the third day be raised again' (Luke 24:5-7).

Mark records the same things mentioned by Matthew and
Luke: the absence of the body, the fact that Jesus had risen,
the invitation to view the empty tomb and the command to tell
the disciples to meet Jesus in Galilee. Mark stresses too that
the good news about Jesus Christ, the Son of God, is now
complete, fulfilled to the letter of Jesus' own predictions about
himself: ' "Don't be alarmed," he said. "You are looking for
Jesus the Nazarene, who was crucified. He has risen! He is
not here. See the place where they laid him" ' (Mark 16:6).

Mark is making the point that the Jesus who has risen was
the same one who had been with the women-folk throughout
his three years' ministry. Indeed, he was the Jesus who came
from 'Nazareth'. Mark, at the very outset of his Gospel, cites
the words of a man possessed by an evil spirit whom Jesus

first healed: 'What do you want with us, Jesus of Nazareth? Have you come to destroy us? I know who you are — the Holy One of God!' (Mark 1:24). Mark is forcefully saying that the words of a demoniac at the beginning of his Gospel and those of a divine messenger at the close are about one and the same person: Jesus of 'Nazareth', incarnate, crucified and risen Lord. His story is now gloriously complete.

Mark alone mentions Peter by name in this report: 'But go, tell his disciples and Peter, "He is going ahead of you into Galilee. There you will see him, just as he told you" ' (Mark 16:7). Why is Peter mentioned in the angel's words? Peter is singled out because Mark earlier records Jesus' predictions of Peter's denial and of their meeting in Galilee:

'You will all fall away,' Jesus told them, 'for it is written:

' "I will strike the shepherd
and the sheep will be scattered."

'But after I have risen, I will go ahead of you into Galilee.'
Peter declared, 'Even if all fall away, I will not.'
'I tell you the truth,' Jesus answered, 'today — yes, tonight — before the cock crows twice you yourself will disown me three times.'
But Peter insisted emphatically, 'Even if I have to die with you, I will never disown you.' And all the others said the same' (Mark 14:27-31).

The love and forgiveness of the risen Lord for Peter is being highlighted. Where would this information about the angel's words most likely have come from, but from Peter himself, wanting to stress his own failings alongside the grace of his Lord's forgiveness? Again, this suggests an intriguing link between Mark and Peter. Was Papias really correct? Is Mark's Gospel, indeed, Peter's memoirs?

What Mark stresses is not just the resurrection of Jesus, which Jesus himself foretold, but the additional prediction to Peter specifically that, after rising from the dead, Jesus would go ahead of the disciples to Galilee and there prove to them beyond all reasonable doubt that he had indeed risen. What a rebuke for Peter! The end of Mark's story again goes right back to the beginning. The Simon whom Jesus called would eventually be a fisher of men, whatever his intervening failure might have been (cf. Mark 1:16-17).

Mark continues his theme from death to resurrection not as an epilogue but as a continuation of the Gospel. The facts are objective, rooted in history in space and time. The facts are also personal. Just as in Jesus' life and death we are challenged personally, so in Jesus' resurrection, along with Peter, we are faced with the same personal confrontation. Mark is not expounding academic theology, but announcing historic gospel fact which challenges us individually. Jesus is a real person, born, crucified and risen. He confronts as sacrificial Saviour and triumphant Lord. Again, in Mark, Jesus steps out of the Gospel and stands before us personally with all his miraculous and absolute claims on our lives.

A young lady faced great trauma in her life. Anxiety, grief, disappointment and uncertainty had shattered her existence. It was like an earthquake in her experience, dislodging all that was firm and stable. She was terribly and sadly alone. A Christian, she turned to God for help, but even he seemed distant. Torn between soul-searching and self-analysis, she did not know what to do. It was a totally different world in which she now lived, so unlike what she had once known. It was unsure, insecure, like a nightmare from which she longed to wake up. It was like stepping from fact into fiction, from reality to fantasy. But it was real life!

She stumbled and wept her way through. She held on to Christ, followed his Word, talked to him in prayer as best she could. Assured of that initial step of faith a number of years before, examining herself at fearful depth, she moved forward in Christian experience. Confidence in her Lord helped to restore confidence in herself as a believer. Christian service developed and increased. The answer to her problem was knowing that Jesus is the same. He is the same yesterday, today, for ever. He is the crucified and risen Master, the sacrificial Saviour and triumphant Lord. He is not dead but alive and alive for evermore. Through the torture of her experience, not the glibness of light emotion, she had learned the truth of the little chorus:

He lives, he lives,
Christ Jesus lives today;
He walks with me and talks with me
Along life's narrow way.
He lives, he lives,
Salvation to impart.
You ask me how I know he lives?
He lives within my heart.

That is the bottom line of Mark's resurrection story. It is continuation, not epilogue. Evidence for the risen Jesus wells up calmly and coolly in these stirring and traumatic facts. Mark is showing that the same Jesus who was crucified is now risen from death and alive for evermore. The truth is not merely historical and factual; it is experiential. If Jesus is alive, he must live within my heart.

Thine be the glory, risen, conquering Son,
Endless is the victory thou o'er death has won;
Angels in bright raiment rolled the stone away,
Kept the folded grave-clothes, where thy body lay.

Thine be the glory, risen, conquering Son,
Endless is the victory thou o'er death has won.

Lo! Jesus meets us, risen from the tomb;
Lovingly he greets us, scatters fear and gloom;
Let the church with gladness hymns of triumph sing,
For her Lord now liveth; death hath lost its sting.

No more we doubt thee, glorious Prince of life;
Life is nought without thee: aid us in our strife;
Make us more than conquerors, through thy deathless
    love:
Bring us safe through Jordan to thy home above.
        (Edmond Budry, 1854-1932. trans. R. Birch Houle,
                                            1875-1939).

Completion, not addition

Mark 16:9-20 is not included in two early manuscripts of the
New Testament, though it is in others. Among those who do
not accept these verses as an original part of Mark's Gospel
are some notable conservative scholars — N. B. Stonehouse,
W. L. Lane and W. Hendriksen. Were these final words a later
addition by someone other than Mark? In favour of this view
the following arguments have been put forward: the abrupt
ending at verse 8 would suit Mark's style and force people to
think; Mary Magdalene is said to appear rather awkwardly in
verse 9 after the reference in verse 1; some unusual words for
Mark occur in verses 9-20.

On the other hand, it is not impossible that Mark could
have added these words after his original composition. Verse
8 is certainly a most abrupt end to the entire Gospel. The reference to Mary Magdalene in verse 9, however, picks up the
threads of the story quite naturally. Indeed, the whole section,

verses 9-20, is an excellent summary of evidence of the resurrection in the other Gospels and is not at all inconsistent with Mark's brief style and clear meaning. The discussion continues.

Whatever conclusion we come to, it is important to recognize that Mark 16:9-20, if not part of Mark's original Gospel, is part of God's Word, similar to that recorded elsewhere in the New Testament. If we believe that the Holy Spirit has superintended not only the writers but the writing of Scripture, we can, with confidence, turn to these verses and learn from them as part of God's inspired Word.

Indeed, as we do look at these verses in detail, we find a parallel with verses 1-8. Just as the earlier verses are a continuation rather than an epilogue to the whole Gospel, so verses 9-20 are a completion rather than an addition to the Gospel. They bring the resurrection story and the Gospel to a fitting conclusion. They trace the progress from unbelief to faith in the person of Christ and emphasize the change from despair to hope through the words of Christ. They show Jesus to be the Son of God and the Son of Man, sacrificial Saviour and triumphant Lord:

> When Jesus rose early on the first day of the week, he appeared first to Mary Magdalene, out of whom he had driven seven demons. She went and told those who had been with him and who were mourning and weeping. When they heard that Jesus was alive and that she had seen him, they did not believe it.
>
> Afterwards Jesus appeared in a different form to two of them while they were walking in the country. These returned and reported it to the rest; but they did not believe them either.
>
> Later Jesus appeared to the Eleven as they were eating; he rebuked them for their lack of faith and their stubborn refusal to believe those who had seen him after he had risen.

He said to them, 'Go into all the world and preach the good news to all creation. Whoever believes and is baptized will be saved, but whoever does not believe will be condemned. And these signs will accompany those who believe: In my name they will drive out demons; they will speak in new tongues; they will pick up snakes with their hands; and when they drink deadly poison, it will not hurt them at all; they will place their hands on sick people, and they will get well.'

After the Lord Jesus had spoken to them, he was taken up into heaven and he sat at the right hand of God. Then the disciples went out and preached everywhere, and the Lord worked with them and confirmed his word by the signs that accompanied it (Mark 16:9-20).

From unbelief to faith

Mary Magdalene

Mary was there among the other ladies on the day of resurrection. Her unbelief showed in her inability to accept that Jesus was alive. Her trust in Jesus was still there. He had cast from her life those seven evil spirits. She could never forget that. Mary, with the rest, was alarmed, bewildered and afraid. Then she meets Jesus in person (Mark 16:1-9). The change is remarkable. She goes and tells the disciples what she has heard and seen (Mark 16:10). Her unbelief becomes faith through meeting the person of the risen Jesus.

Both Matthew and Luke mention the meeting between the risen Christ and Mary Magdalene, but John gives the fullest account of this. She meets the risen Christ near the tomb, fails to recognize him and then, as he calls her by name, she gladly and warmly responds to her Master (John 20:10-18). Mark's

summary plucks out a feature from Mary's lurid past, her erstwhile demon-possession (cf. Luke 8:2), and then shows her
glorious future as a vital witness of the resurrection of Christ
(Mark 16:9-11). Clearly, the emphasis is on her journey from
fearful disbelief to renewed faith.

The two on the road to Emmaus

The two walking in the country have a similar experience.
Jesus appears to them in 'a different form'. They return and
report it to the rest, who do not believe them either (Mark
16:12-13). What does 'a different form' mean? A resurrection
body not immediately recognizable, a 'traveller' like Mary's
'gardener'? Luke picks up that point in his narrative. Jesus is
not a ghost. He invites the disciples to touch him. He eats a
piece of broiled fish before them (Luke 24:37-43). How clear
the proof, says Mark, for even in 'a different form' Jesus the
triumphant Lord is Jesus the crucified Saviour.

Luke tells that story of the two on the Emmaus road (Luke
24:13-33). It seems reasonable to take this as an enlarged ver-
sion of Mark's tale of the 'two'. What a wealth of detail is in
Luke's account — their dispirited hearts, their initial lack of
recognition of Jesus, their burning hearts on having Moses
and the prophets expounded to them by Christ, the thrill of
recognizing Jesus as that Christ in the breaking of bread, their
hurried return to Jerusalem and then their buoyant witness to
the Eleven! What does Mark pick from that information in his
summary? The puzzlement of the Emmaus disciples about
Jesus' identity and their spirited report to the disbelieving disciples. Mark, in this summary of the experience of these 'two',
does precisely what he did with Mary Magdalene! He recalls
their unbelieving past and portrays their transformed future.
The 'two' encountering the risen Jesus move from bewilder-
ing unbelief to sure faith.

The Eleven

The effect of the news of the resurrection on the Eleven is put
in the same way by Mark. They believe neither Mary nor the
two travellers (Mark 16:11,13). Jesus appears to them while
they are eating (Mark 16:14). He rebukes their lack of faith
and their reluctance to accept the evidence of witnesses, who
had seen him risen (Mark 16:14). The Eleven are eventually
persuaded. They go out and preach everywhere (Mark 16:20).

Again, Mark summarizes briefly what the other Gospel
writers say at length. Luke records fully how the Emmaus disciples and the Eleven recognized Jesus during a meal (Luke
24:31,35,36-43). John describes in detail how Jesus rebuked
Thomas and Peter for their lack of faith (John 20:24-29; 21:1-
23). Luke depicts the disciples in Jerusalem, joyfully and con-
tinually worshipping God in the temple (Luke 24:52-53). Mark
concisely presents this data to show how the Eleven moved
from stubborn unbelief to active faith through the person of
the risen Jesus.

In each of these cases there is incredulity and a reluctance
to accept the testimony of others. Can it really be Jesus, or is
it a gardener, a traveller or a ghost? Eventually, belief comes
through the manifestation of the person of Jesus himself, different from before, yet the same person. He is still the revealed Messiah, the mysterious God-man, the divine yet human Son of God, but now risen from the dead.

From despair to hope

The process is not simply from unbelief to faith but from despair to hope. It is the *words* of Jesus which bring about the
transformation.

Mary finds the disciples in despair, 'mourning and weeping' (Mark 16:10). Jesus commands them to preach the gospel throughout the world, to all creation. As they do, people will believe, be baptized and be saved. Those who do not believe will be condemned. Signs will accompany those who believe: the exorcism of demons, speaking in new tongues, picking up snakes, drinking deadly poison with no ill effect and the laying of hands on the sick resulting in healing (Mark 16:15-18). Through these words of Jesus' Great Commission the disciples move from despair to hope. They go out and preach everywhere (Mark 16:20). What a change from mourning and weeping!

The place

Mark shows what the future place of the disciples' activities is to be as they serve the risen Jesus. The parameters for preaching the good news are 'all the world' and 'all creation' (Mark 16:15). How wide Mark's presentation of Jesus commission is! Matthew depicts Jesus urging his followers to make disciples of 'all nations' (Matt. 28:19). Luke recalls Jesus indicating that repentance and forgiveness would be preached in his name 'to all nations, beginning at Jerusalem' and that they were witnesses of these things (Luke 24:47-48).

Mark demonstrates our responsibility as believers to witness to Jesus wherever we may be and in whatever way possible. Home, school, work, leisure are all fields of service. Every person Christians come into contact with is their mission-field and a legitimate target for the claims of our Master. Not only lip but life should carry the thrust of that testimony. The whole wide world for Jesus is his parting command to his followers: 'Go into all the world and preach the good news to all creation' (Mark 16:15).

The policy

The specific policy by which this activity is carried out is also emphasized by Mark. Jesus commands his disciples to 'preach the good news' to all creation (Mark 16:16). We are literally to 'herald the gospel'. Ours is the task of announcing with dignity, solemnity and joy the story of Jesus Christ, the Son of God. The end in view of such a policy is that people 'believe' and as a result are 'saved', or alternatively, do not believe and will be 'condemned': 'Whoever believes and is baptized will be saved, but whoever does not believe will be condemned' (Mark 16:16).

The power

The feature most stressed by Mark in Jesus' commission is the *power* of this activity. Mark uses the ordinance of baptism and the signs accompanying those who believe to underline this power. This presentation of Jesus' commission is peculiar to Mark: 'Whoever believes and is baptized will be saved, but whoever does not believe will be condemned. And these signs will accompany those who believe: In my name they will drive out demons; they will speak in new tongues; they will pick up snakes with their hands; and when they drink deadly poison, it will not hurt them at all; they will place their hands on sick people, and they will get well' (Mark 16:16-18).

Matthew mentions baptism in this context also. In making 'disciples of all nations' and 'teaching them to obey everything', Jesus has commanded the eleven disciples that they are to baptize them 'in the name of the Father and of the Son and of the Holy Spirit' (Matt. 28:19). The 'name' of the triune God, in or into which the person is to be baptized, recalls the power of the salvation illustrated by that ordinance. It also recalls the contrast mentioned in all the Gospels between John the Baptist baptizing in water and Jesus the Messiah baptizing with the Holy Spirit. The power is not located in the ordinance itself but in what it points to. The signs and seals of the gospel are always subordinate and subservient to the word of the gospel.

Christ's words do not teach that baptism is necessary to salvation, but depict the divine power and initiative in salvation. Those who believe and are baptized are saved; those who do not believe are condemned, whether baptized or unbaptized. Otherwise, he would have put it like this: 'Whoever believes and is baptized will be saved, but whoever does not believe and is not baptized will be condemned.' The form of Jesus' words, as recorded by Mark, emphasizes the truth that baptism is only the sign of faith, not an indispensable substitute for faith.

Mark mentions five signs accompanying those who believe as further proof of the power of the gospel. Of these signs at least three, and possibly four, occur elsewhere in the New Testament:

power to expel demons	Matt. 10:1; Mark 9:38; Luke 10:17; Acts 5:16; 8:7; 16:18; 19:12
ability to speak in new tongues	Acts 2:4; 10:46; 1 Cor.12:10, 28,30; 14:1-25
ability to pick up serpents	possibly Luke 10:19; Acts 28:3-5
gift of being able to drink deadly poison without being hurt	no New Testament evidence
power to place hands on sick who will then recover	Matt. 10:1; Acts 5:16; 8:7; 19:12

However, as with baptism, they are only signs confirming the words of Jesus. The gospel, or words of Jesus, the name and power of Jesus are the important things. Belief in those is basic to salvation. The signs are subordinate to the Word, meaningful and confirmatory, but still secondary to the gospel: 'The Lord worked with them and confirmed his word by the signs that accompanied it' (Mark 16:20).

Luke recalls how Jesus encouraged his disciples to wait in Jerusalem until they had been clothed with power from on high (Luke 24:49). He then goes on in Acts to outline how this power came and these signs were demonstrated (Acts 2:1-10). Mark too emphasizes the great power which Jesus' words brought. The disciples move from deep despair to assured hope through the *words* of the risen Jesus, the dynamic Prophet, controversial Teacher, the Son of God.

From resurrection to ascension

The story of Jesus' ascension is found at the end of both Mark and Luke and at the beginning of the Acts of the Apostles (Mark 16:19; Luke 24:50-51; Acts 1:9-11). All three accounts speak of Jesus as being 'taken up' from the disciples in the direction of heaven or the sky. Luke in his Gospel describes the disciples, immediately after the ascension, as worshipping Jesus, returning from Bethany to Jerusalem with great joy and staying at the temple praising God (Luke 24:53). In the Acts Luke gives a yet more detailed account. As the disciples looked up into the sky at the ascending Jesus, they were directed by two men in white standing beside them: 'Why do you stand here looking into the sky? This same Jesus, who has been taken from you into heaven, will come back in the same way you have seen him go into heaven' (Acts 1:9-11; cf. Luke 24:4-8).

The disciples then return to Jerusalem from the Mount of Olives — a Sabbath day's walk, or about three-quarters of a mile — and go to an upper room where the Eleven, the women and Jesus' mother and brothers continue together in prayer (Acts 1:12-14).

'After the Lord Jesus had spoken to them, he was taken up into heaven and he sat at the right hand of God. Then the disciples went out and preached everywhere, and the Lord worked with them and confirmed his word by signs that accompanied it' (Mark 16:19-20). Mark is highlighting two features in particular: Christ's position and the disciples' activity. The risen, ascended Jesus is now in the place of privilege and authority at God's right hand. Yet, in an amazing way, he is still present with his disciples, by his Spirit, confirming his Word by accompanying signs, as they preach everywhere. This summary takes in much of the early history of the church as recorded by Luke in Acts. For Mark, just as *power* characterized Christ's *words* after the resurrection, so his *presence* characterized Christ's *work* after the ascension.

Mark completes his Gospel in the same concise way that he began it. The risen, ascended Christ continues to work. The gospel is complete in Christ's finished work, but not concluded in its effects. It is gloriously open-ended and continuing. Redemption accomplished is now redemption being applied. Jesus suffering Servant, majestic King, sacrificial Saviour, triumphant Lord, Son of Man, crucified, risen, ascended, is now at the Father's right hand. The beginning of the gospel of Jesus Christ is now at an end. But the end is really only the beginning for all mankind.

> He is gone — beyond the skies!
> A cloud receives him from our eyes:
> Gone beyond the highest height
> Of mortal gaze or angel's flight,

Through the veils or time and space
Passed into the holiest place —
All the toil, the sorrow done,
All the battle fought and won.

He is gone: and we remain
In this world of sin and pain;
In the void which he has left
On this earth, of him bereft,
We have still his work to do,
We can still his path pursue,
Seek him both in friend and foe,
In ourselves his image show.

He is gone: we heard him say,
'Good that I should go away.'
Gone is that dear form and face,
But not gone his present grace;
Though himself no more we see,
Comfortless we cannot be:
No! His Spirit still is ours,
Quickening, freshening all our powers.

He is gone: but we once more
Shall behold him as before,
In the heaven of heavens the same
As on earth he went and came:
In the many mansions there
Place for us he will prepare;
In that world unseen, unknown,
He and we shall yet be one.

(Arthur Penrhyn Stanley, 1815-81)